The Power To Change

Sermons For Lent And Easter Cycle B First Lesson Texts

Durwood L. Buchheim

CSS Publishing Company, Inc.
Lima, Ohio

THE POWER TO CHANGE

Copyright © 1993 by
The CSS Publishing Company, Inc.
Lima, Ohio

Library of Congress Cataloging-in-Publication Data

Buchheim, Durwood, 1923-
    The power to change : sermons for Lent-Easter : cycle B, first lesson texts / by Durwood Buchheim.
       p.   cm.
    ISBN 1-55673-612-6
    1. Lenten sermons. 2. Eastertide — Sermons. 3. Sermons, American. 4. Bible. O.T. — Sermons. I. Title.
BV4277.B77   1993
252'.62—dc20   93-18008
                                               CIP

9337 / ISBN 1-55673-612-6   PRINTED IN U.S.A.

Preface

Most of the sermons in this little volume were preached to the members of Bethlehem Lutheran Congregation, Royal, Iowa, and Holy Trinity Lutheran Church, Dubuque, Iowa. Their affirming support made my three month interim ministry in their midst a delightful experience.

But our sermons are nurtured by many experiences. I want to acknowledge with gratitude the encouragement I received from members of Trinity American Lutheran Church, Waterloo, Iowa, and St. Paul's Lutheran Church, Waverly, Iowa. I owe much to these people for the privilege of being their preacher and pastor.

Perhaps my greatest debt is to Dr. G. E. Melchert who instilled confidence in his inexperienced assistant and demonstrated via word and example the importance of disciplined sermon preparation.

Durwood Buchheim
Lent, 1993

Table Of Contents

Ash Wednesday
Joel 2:1-2; 12-17a

We Do Not Have To
Stay The Way We Are!

"Have I been with you so long, and yet you do not know me, Philip?" (John 14:9) So Jesus responded to Philip's question about wanting to know and sense the presence of God.

It is a good question for all of us as we once again make our Lenten journey to Easter. How would you answer if asked to share your thoughts about God? What thoughts come to mind when we think about God? Do we take the time to think about God? Do we believe there is a God? Are we more confident this year than last, that there is a God who knows and is concerned about us? Does our belief in God make any difference in our lifestyles?

Amid the many, busy and distracting events of our lives, the quiet hours of Lenten worship are certainly needed. It is a needed time for solitude, for reflection and meditation as we journey through our particular wilderness to Easter. Yes, to look at how we are doing and why; yes, to evaluate our relationship with God. Lent is that traditional time of the year when we are urged to probe into the deeper corners of our being. Lent is a time "to be still and know that I am God."

But one would hope that our quiet time with God would have some explosive results. Our journey to Easter should not be all peace and tranquility:

7

Lent is a season for crash helmets. It is a season for deep self-examination, intense emotion, purging the soul and reorienting life by discovering anew not only what sort of power it is "we so blithely invoke," but also about the dark powers which are at work in human experience. Lent began as a time when candidates for baptism would like gladiators preparing for battle, discipline themselves for the spiritual warfare ahead. [1]

This year we are making our pilgrimage to Easter through readings from the Old Testament. Most of these readings are centered on or around the "covenant" that God made with Israel. A covenant is an agreement or contract that God initiates. Through the covenant, God speaks and the people of the covenant listen. It is because God has spoken that we know what God wants. Covenant thinking directs our thought to God and what God has done for us and what God expects from us. To have our thoughts directed to God, to listen to God is more helpful than intense navel gazing which can lead to the problem of our gospel reading for today, and that is spiritual pride. But lifting our eyes and seeing the faithful activity of God on our behalf can pull us out of ourselves into more faithful, useful and joyful living.

We begin our Lenten journey with the prophet Joel. We know very little about this prophet. Joel's book contains no calendar references and it is completely silent about kings or empires. Yet the style and content of the book would suggest that Joel is one of the later prophets, probably living and working about 400 years B.C., during the time of the Persian Empire. Chronologically (because of its late date) this is not the best place to begin our Lenten sermons on the Old Testament. But with its clear and ringing call for repentance, this book makes a good spiritual entry point for the season of Lent. Because of this clear and needed call to repentance, many Christian denominations are hearing this text at their Ash Wednesday services.

The book of Joel is filled with references to a great and destructive plague of locusts. He paints a picture of utter

8

destruction that is left by these hungry pests. They come in huge clouds, sweeping over the whole land, and making gardens and fields like a desert.

> *Fire devours before them,*
> *and behind them a flame burns.*
> *The land is like the garden of Eden*
> *before them,*
> *but after them a desolate wilderness,*
> *and nothing escapes them* ... (2:3)

The prophet saw in this terrible calamity a forewarning of the coming day of judgment, the day of the Lord. Disasters of this magnitude have a theological meaning for this prophet of God. It is not just nature speaking, but the God above and behind nature. In this terrible locust invasion the people of God are being warned about the seriousness of their situation. This prophet sees calamities as a vivid reminder to return to God in repentance.

Joel follows in the time-honored tradition of the prophets of old. Take Amos, for example, when he preached this warning to his people:

> *"I gave you cleanness of teeth in*
> *all your cities*
> *and lack of bread in all your places,*
> *yet you did not return to me,"*
> *says the Lord.*
> *"And I also withheld the rain from you*
> *when there were yet three*
> *months to the harvest;*
> *I would send rain upon another city;*
> *one field would be rained upon,*
> *and the field on which it did not rain withered;*
> *so two or three cities wandered to one city*
> *to drink water, and were not satisfied;*
> *yet you did not return to me,"*
> *says the Lord.* (4:6-8)

In our text for this Ash Wednesday worship, we read the call to repentance in these words:

> *"Yet even now," says the Lord,*
> *"return to me with all your heart,*
> *with fasting, with weeping, and with mourning;*
> *and rend your hearts and not your garments."* (vv. 12-13)

The consistent message of all scripture is that the only way to escape God's judgment is through repentance.

Fasting, weeping and mourning were the usual expressions of repentance, but they became a pious performance rather than "a broken and a contrite heart." (Psalm 51:17) And so the dramatic call, "rend your hearts and not your garments."

"Heart" in Hebrew understanding has more to do with one's will than one's affections. To "rend the heart" is the call to change. It is a strong exhortation to subdue the will. The "tearing of garments" was part of the usual ritual for mourning. (2 Samuel 1:11) It was a visible expression of grief and subject to misuse. "Look how sorry I am!" "Rending one's garments" is a way of repenting loudly so all people can see what great "repenters" we are. It is repentance growing out of pride. Both our Old and New Testament lessons for today speak against a repentance for show.

Of course, it is also easy to "rend one's garments." We can pray and fast and give up things for Lent. We can for a period of six weeks even show compassion for the poor and maybe increase our contributions. But frequently these efforts are only skin deep and once again the result is a kind of cosmetic piety whereby we fool others and maybe even ourselves.

But how can we "rend our hearts?" How can we change our way of thinking? How can we change the direction of our lives? How can we change our basic attitude, the orientation of our lives? That is what true repentance is about and that is what it means to "rend our hearts."

The old story is told of the Sunday school teacher who asked her class of boys, "What must we do to receive the forgiveness of sin?'' One of her boys replied, ''Well, first you must sin!'' Here is one of the big hurdles for the spirit of true repentance and that is our need for it. The concept of sin does not have much going for it in our modern climate and its idolatrous desire for self-affirmation. We may have made some mistakes or bad decisions because we were wrongly positioned in our family, but surely these little things couldn't separate one from God?

Several years ago the country was caught up in the drama of an 18-month-old girl being trapped in a deep and narrow abandoned well. For three days the country watched and waited as television crews in pictures and words reported this race with death. But finally the second shaft was finished and the little girl was saved — cold and hurt — but alive. And the nation, with parents and rescuers wept with joy.

However, a few months later much of this good will and joy changed into envy, hate, greed and suspicion. Movie people came to the little Texas town and groups began to fight among themselves as to how the story should be told and who was to get the credit and receive the profits.

Such is the power of sin. That sin is original in us is not a popular idea. I would much rather deal with my sinful activities than a sinful ''me.'' But the truth of the matter is that I am not sinful because I do bad things, but I do bad things because ''by nature I am sinful and unclean.''

One of the most vivid and persuasive examples of sin in our century is the Holocaust. Here sin was engaged in the unbelievable task of destroying the people of God. It is easy to focus on the demon Hitler, but the truth is that most of the world was involved. Hatred for the Jews has been around for a long, long time and we Christians are guilty of promoting and feeding these fears and suspicions.

We read in Elie Wiesel's novel, *The Oath*, these words, ''With every approaching Easter, the Jews tremble.'' Robert McAfee Brown, professor emeritus at Pacific School of Religion in Berkeley, California, makes these comments concerning Wiesel's observation:

"Why? Because as Good Friday and Easter approach, Christians have frequently taken up cudgels against Jews, holding them responsible for Jesus' death, and feeling called upon to avenge that death by killing Jews. Persecutions, pogroms, forced conversions, mob violence, burning of ghettos — all of the tools of the anti-Semitic trade have historically been given license for expression the closer the Christian year gets to Easter. 'Born in suffering,' Wiesel writes elsewhere, 'Christianity became a source and pretext of suffering to others.' "[2]

The Holocaust insanity was accomplished by well-educated people growing up in a well-endowed cultural, technological and Christian environment. And even more frightening, the world found many reasons to turn its back on this insane event.

Such is the power of our fallen nature. We look for scapegoats. The presence of sin enables us to take credit for our own success and comfort because we are "better" people, and to blame poverty and suffering on the lazy, sinful victims. We look for evil in other people and in other nations, all the time ignoring the beam in our own eyes. We know that the Bible tells us "that all have sinned," but we all know that there are differences in sinners. We are not as bad as most!

Do we need to be reminded of Isaiah's admonition, "I am a man of unclean lips, and I dwell in the midst of a people of unclean lips)" (6:5) Do we need to be reminded that when it comes to sinners, the Bible has two basic distinctions — repentant, or unrepentant?

Repentance is coming to our senses like the prodigal son and seeing ourselves as we really are — warts and all. Repentance is facing up to the powerful desires within us to deceive — to deceive others and ourselves.

But repentance is not only recognition, it is also repudiation. I like the insight by the old revivalist, Gypsy Smith, who said that the difference between conversion and repentance is the difference between waking up and getting up! Frequently getting caught will produce feelings of remorse, anguish, regret and sorrow, but unhappiness is not repentance.

12

Genuine repentance means that the direction of our lives has changed. It means we have come to our senses and we arise and return to our God. We ourselves must be changed!

And we can't do this on our own. We can "rend our garments, but not our hearts." Our bonds of captivity are too strong to break on our own. In our sin, we simply do not have the power to direct our own repentance. Power to repent comes from God's decision to save. I doubt very much if the prodigal son would have gone home to an elder brother, but going home to a loving father is an altogether different matter. The relationship of love makes all the difference.

So also with the people of Israel. Their prophet Joel not only tells them to "rend your hearts and not your garments" but goes on to say:

> *Return to the Lord, your God,*
> *for he is gracious and merciful,*
> *slow to anger, and abounding in steadfast love,*
> *and repents of evil.* (v. 13)

The people of God were reminded of their history, a history of their faithful, loving God. A God who called them into a covenant relationship. A God who patiently put up with their whining and complaining unfaithfulness. Yes, that is their history — the history of steadfast love continuing to love a stiff-necked and stubborn people. God is not against a sinful people. Rather, God's vision and purpose is one of mercy and promise.

God is not a harsh judge looking and waiting for us to make mistakes and then pounce on us. Joel's God is a God of mercy. Jesus' God is one of compassion and mercy. Sometimes the message of Lent and Easter can come across as though the cross was erected on Calvary to please God. But this is a pagan idea. Christ was not nailed to the cross to change God's heart, rather it was just the other way around. The cross is there because "God was in Christ reconciling us into himself."

13

The Calvary event happened because "God so loved the world, he sent his Son."

Here is power to change the direction of our lives. Here is power to grow in faith. The history of the people of God and our own history warns us not to underestimate the power of sin in our lives. In Matthew's gospel the warning is given so all can understand it, "For where your treasure is, there will your heart be also." My life will follow that which I believe to be the most important. This warning needs to be heeded, but it would be even more disastrous to push God out of our history and our lives and ignore God's power to change us. God's love can pull us out of ourselves. God's love can become our "treasure." In the relationship there is power to change.

We do not have to stay the way we are.

------

[1] The Editors, "Forward," *Journal for Preachers,* (Lent, 1986, p. 1).

[2] Robert McAfee Brown, "Jewish Contributions to a Christian Lent: The Impact of Elie Wiesel," *Perspectives,* (Feb. 1986, p. 4).

Lent 1
Genesis 9:8-17

The Covenant
Of Amazing Grace

"The earth is degenerating these days. Bribery and cor-
ruption abound. Children no longer mind their parents.
Everyone wants to write a book, and it is evident the end
of the world is fast approaching."[1]

Sounds like the evening news or tomorrow's headlines,
doesn't it? The truth is that this description of society was
found inscribed on an Assyrian tablet dated 2000 B.C.

Jurgen Moltmann, professor of theology at the University
of Tubingen, West Germany, shares this modern observation
concerning our anxious age:

> *The nightmare of Armageddon has replaced the politi-*
> *cal vision of hope for life, freedom and justice through-*
> *out the world: The monster of the nuclear apocalypse is*
> *felt everywhere. "Apocalypse Now" is not only a film*
> *title these years; people everywhere are hearing the bells*
> *of the world's clock ring for the last time. "Five minutes*
> *to twelve" is a running introduction to new terror reports,*
> *be it about environmental pollution, about methods of*
> *mass extermination or about the starvation of millions*
> *in the Third World.*[2]

We are at the beginning of the season of Lent. This is a
precious time of the year for many Christians, our annual

15

journey to Easter. Through the gospel reading for this Sunday, we are reminded that this journey begins in the wilderness. The business of living has been compared to a wilderness journey. We know that wildernesses can foster the spirit of worry and anxiety. Our age has been called the "age of anxiety."

So it seems that the basic worries of life never change, but neither do the promises of God! Once again we will hear these promises through some great and memorable stories from the Old Testament. Appropriately we begin our Lenten journey in the first book of the Old Testament, which is known by its Greek name, Genesis, which means beginning or coming into being. One of the great emphases of this book of beginnings is the promise of God.

The conclusion to the powerful story of Noah and the flood contains such a promise.

This promise of hope comes at a hopeless time. In the first six chapters of Genesis we see the progress of sin, like a fast growing cancer moving into and corrupting all society. The fall of Adam and Eve set in motion a chain reaction of evil and the whole universe was infected. In this long period of time things went from bad to worse. Cain murdered his brother Abel. Lamech introduced polygamy. Unnatural marriage alliances were formed.

We read in the sixth chapter of Genesis, "The Lord saw that the wickedness of humankind was great in the earth, and that every inclination of the thoughts of their heart was only evil continually. And the Lord was sorry that he made humankind on the earth, and it grieved him to his heart." Sin is unchecked and the universe is moving toward disaster. When evil becomes a way of life and decency long forgotten and absent, the pressure for moral justice brings with it forces of destruction. The flood is the judgment of God, but also the inevitable fruit of the growing evil of humanity.

But equally important, God demonstrates mercy by delivering a remnant with whom a new beginning is made. It is important to note that God's judgment comes from a heart of sorrow and not from a vindictive, revengeful spirit. The ultimate aim of God's wrath is repentance and restoration, never revenge and destruction. This hope-filled purpose of God is shared in the promise of our text, "I establish my covenant with you, that never again shall all flesh be cut off by the waters of a flood, and never again shall there be a flood to destroy the earth."

Since God's promise is contained in God's "covenant," it is important that we have some understanding as to the meaning of this rather strange word — at least strange to modern ears. Nevertheless, try to stay tuned to my wavelength, because this is an important biblical word and it will be back time and time again in the Lenten texts that are to come.

To ease us into these covenant waters, think agreement for the word covenant.

There are three main agreements described in the first five books of the Bible: 1) The agreement with Abraham, where God says, "I am God Almighty; walk before me, and be blameless. And I will make my covenant between me and you, and will multiply you exceedingly;" 2) The agreement with the children of Israel made at Mount Sinai, where God says, "You have seen what I did to the Egyptians, and how I bore you on eagles' wings and brought you to myself. Now, therefore, if you will obey my voice and keep my covenant, you shall be my own possession among all peoples; for all the earth is mine, and you shall be to me a kingdom of priests and a holy nation." (Exodus 19:4-6)

These important agreements (covenants) are made by God with the people of Israel. It is God's redemptive initiative that establishes these agreements. They are agreements (covenants) of grace. Out of these agreements of grace come the obligation of God's people to live obediently in these "agreed-upon" relationships.

In our text for today, we have the third God-established agreement. However, this agreement is not made only with the people of Israel, but with all humankind. It could be described as God's "amazing grace" agreement never again to destroy the earth by flood. This is the promise of hope in divine preservation.

It is the promise of a new beginning that is the foundation of this hope. God's promises lead to a new future. Just as God once began with Adam and Eve, God now begins with the family of Noah. This new beginning does not take place in a new paradise, a new garden of Eden. People are not magically transformed into goodness. We are still sinful. Sin has brought changes into God's creation with which we still have to live and contend. But God loves us! The great hope here is that God has not quit on us or on creation. God still rules. God's promises and commands still hold. God remains lovingly concerned about us and the world we live in. After the flood (judgment), humanity is permitted to begin anew, with new promises and blessings.

The first sign of that promise of hope was the single olive leaf which the dove brought back to the ark. In our text this hope is expressed in the covenant relationship, "I establish my covenant with you, that never again shall all flesh be cut off by the waters of a flood ..." (v. 11)

God's covenants (remember, we are talking about God's agreements) are guaranteed by signs. In the case of this amazing grace covenant, the sign is the rainbow. The rainbow, which appears after storms, is a fitting and beautiful symbol of hope. Through the chaos that the sin-storm has caused in our world, God is still present with a patient love that promises never again to destroy the earth with a catastrophe like the flood.

We have hope because our God is a gracious and patient God. In the covenant with Noah, God demonstrates love for all living creatures. In a later time, Peter makes the connection with Christian baptism, as he recalls for us the days of Noah and how eight persons were saved through the water. (1 Peter 3:20) As the flood cleansed the world from the effects of sin, so the waters of baptism cleanse us. In this great hope there is power to face the stormy seas of life.

We have to be careful here that our faith in God's promises, which are the foundation of our hope, do not make us "passive" Christians. This happens when we substitute faith for our human responsibility. When this happens faith becomes an escape hatch and we become resigned to our fate — what will be, will be. This kind of faith is not childlike but childish and irresponsible. We humans now have the power to annihilate ourselves. The covenant with Noah is no guarantee that God somehow is going to limit our power to destroy ourselves if we want to.

In the real world hope also has to do battle with the spirit of cynicism. Cynics see little or no hope for our time. On the other hand this kind of hopeless spirit can and does lead to violence and destruction — a what-have-we-got-to-lose attitude. On the other hand the cynical spirit is not far removed from the spirit of eat, drink and be merry. Just leave us alone. Eventually the world will be destroyed, either slowly but surely through pollution, or quickly by the bomb. So leave us alone to enjoy what remains and what is left of a world that is beyond salvation. What else makes sense but to live for the moment and to live for ourselves?

But Christian hope is not to be found in a blind faith that retreats from reality and certainly not in a cynical denial of hope. Faith holds together in tension, both our experiences and our expectations.[3] We long for justice and desire a God who will guarantee it, but this also makes us vulnerable to irresponsible escapism and false religious comfort. We come back to the primary basis of our hope which is God's grace and not our experiences. "Now faith is the assurance of things hoped for, the conviction of things not seen." (Hebrews 11:1)

For the Christian, the most powerful symbol for "assurance of things hoped for" is the cross of Christ. The cross is the center of our journey through life. It reminds us of struggle, the struggle for faith that we might have hope. But like the story of the flood, only with a how much more the cross of Christ reveals the continuing costly and amazing grace of God. Once more the season of Lent invites us to be still and trust this grace, for in this amazing grace is our hope. In this hope there is power to live the purposeful life.

19

Again quoting Moltmann:

"The Christian hope is not directed for a happy end of world history. ... In the moment of deathly danger, God's stories in the Bible speak and awaken hope where otherwise there is nothing else to hope. The memories of being rescued from disaster do not deny disaster. They speak of the God who made the hopeless disaster of his people his own and who led his people out of it. ... The answer of hope to the threatening danger of annihilation is the life with a raised head and unequivocal self-commitment. And if the end of the world would happen tomorrow, 'Let us plant our apple tree today.' (M. Luther)"[4]

---

[1]The source of this quotation is unknown to the author.

[2]Jurgen Moltmann, "God, Hope, and Nuclear Catastrophe," (*Perspectives,* April 1988, pp. 7-10).

[3]Douglas John Hall, *Lighten Our Darkness*, (Philadelphia, Westminster Press, 1976). I am indebted to this book and other writings (and lectures) by Hall on the matter of realistic hope in our time.

[4]*Ibid,* Jurgen Moltmann, p. 10.

God's Great Promise To Sarah!

Confession is good for one's soul. You are about to hear a personal confession.

My mother, who was a pioneer farmer's wife, was treated as a second-class citizen. Oh, she had the right to vote and was secretary for our school district for most of my young, adult life and was in charge of family finances. She commanded respect from husband and children — yet in no way did she receive equal treatment. In my childhood on the farm, men had to do certain things, most women had to be able to do (and in many cases did) everything. My mother, who was the oldest in her family, worked outside the house about as much as inside. Consequently her life was tough and full of hard work. There were very few moments in her life when she wasn't busy at something. (In certain areas of our world women still work double, or even triple the hours of men.) My mother was boxed into not just a Martha role but also the manly role. She was not just responsible for housekeeping and hospitality but had to fill in wherever help was needed. And most of us assumed that was the way it was and was meant to be. I didn't know it then, but a morning prayer in the Hebrew tradition described my attitude and feelings quite accurately, "I thank God that I was not born a woman."

21

My mother handled this "second class" business very well. I suspect she too believed this was the way it was supposed to be. After all what are mothers for? But it was a most unfair and unjust arrangement and I am ashamed at how long it took me to see and begin to appreciate just how unfair and unjust our society has treated women. Consequently, I have no problem with the doctrine of original sin. I have seen too much evidence of it in my own life.

All of this came to mind as I worked on this familiar Abraham story. I have heard and preached many sermons on Abraham. In my confirmation classes, Abraham was a well-publicized hero. The Bible makes much over Abraham. History looks upon him much in the same light. Christians call him the father of believers. Jews proudly call him their father. Even Mohammedans make much of him. All of this is in order, for with Abraham a new nation began.

Abraham and his relatives demonstrated great trust in God. They were the recipients of a promise that seemed a long way from fulfillment. Their greatness consisted in the fact that they "looked forward to a city that has foundations, whose architect and builder is God." (Hebrews 11:10)

But Abraham wasn't alone in following these promises of God. Sarah, his wife, was also with him. But I have never heard a sermon on Sarah, nor have I preached one. Maybe out of guilt, or maybe out of respect for the memory of my mother's hard, but useful life, this sermon is going to be about one of the great women of the Bible, Sarah.[1]

In our text for today, we are in the Abraham/Sarah stories. In the first 11 of this 50-chapter book we have the story of creation and the beginning history of humanity. In these first chapters we go from the Adam and Eve stories, the power and progress of sin, the story of Noah and the flood, to the tower of Babel and finally to the family of Terah and the birth of Abraham.

The remaining 39 chapters of Genesis describe the lives of four generations of descendants of the family of Terah: 1) Abraham and Sarah, 2) Isaac and Rebekah, 3) Jacob and Leah and Rachel, 4) the stories of Joseph and the 12 tribes of Israel.

The book of Genesis is our only source of information about Sarah, but she is an important part of the Abraham story. She and her husband migrate to the promised land of Canaan. But because of a severe drought they move south to Egypt. Then comes this strange incident which reveals much about Sarah and her husband Abraham, for Abraham says to his wife Sarah:

> *"I know well that you are a woman beautiful in appearance; and when the Egyptians see you, they will say, 'This is his wife;' then they will kill me, but they will let you live. Say you are my sister, so that it may go well with me because of you, and that my life may be spared on your account."* (Genesis 12:11-13)

We know that the cowardly plan worked. Sarah agreed. She became Pharaoh's mistress and things went well for Abraham. He acquired much wealth. But Pharaoh didn't fare so well. He and his household were afflicted with plagues. Once he discovered the reason behind all his bad luck, Sarah and Abraham were reunited and sent on their way. In this story both the Pharaoh and Sarah came out looking much better than Abraham.

The next significant event in Sarah's life has to do with the truth that "Sarah, Abram's wife, bore him no children." (Genesis 16:1) According to the customs of that time it was right and generous of Sarah to be willing to let her maid, Hagar bear a child to her husband. Children born of such a union were accepted as the children, not of the maid but of the wife, by adoption. Sarah was determined to have an heir, even if through a concubine.

Hagar is the slave woman in this story, but she too, is nobody's fool or doormat. She comes across as a sturdy, independent woman, willing and able to fight for the rights of her son. Commentaries make much over the jealousy between these two women. We hear little about their strength, concern

23

and generosity. Yet in an honest and careful reading of Genesis, women are seen as important and respected participants in God's covenant promises.

We now come to our text for today and God's promise to Sarah:

> *"As for Sarah your wife, you shall not call her Sarai, but Sarah shall be her name. I will bless her, and moreover I will give you a son by her. I will bless her and she shall give rise to nations; kings of peoples shall come from her."* (vv. 15-16)

Here we are told that Sarai's name is changed to Sarah, which means "princess." We should also note the specific promise to Sarah; she will be a mother of nations; kings of people shall come from her!

What follows in her life is described by preacher and author, Fredrick Buechner:

> *"The place to start is with a woman laughing. ... The old woman's name is Sarah, of course, and the old man's name is Abraham .... They are laughing because with another part of themselves they know it would take a fool to believe it. ... They are laughing because if by some crazy chance it should just happen to come true, then they would really have something to laugh about."*[2]

We read the climax of this great event in these stirring words:

> *"The Lord dealt with Sarah as he had said, and the Lord did for Sarah as he had promised. Sarah conceived and bore Abraham a son in his old age, at the time of which God had spoken to him."* (Genesis 21:1-2)

It seems that God not only approved of their laughter, but probably joined in, for God gave instructions that this miracle baby was to be named Isaac which means "laughter."

It is strange that the mother is not mentioned as preparations were made for the sacrifice of her long-awaited son. The Genesis story is silent about the obvious anguish and suffering that Sarah must have endured.

We hear no more about Sarah until this significant information in Genesis 23:

> *"Sarah lived 127 years; this was the length of Sarah's life. And Sarah died at Kiriath-arba (that is, Hebron) in the land of Canaan, and Abraham went in to mourn for Sarah and to weep for her . . . Abrahɑⁿ buried Sarah his wife in the cave of the field of N pelach facing Mamre (that is, Hebron) in the land of Canaan."* (vv. 1ff)

Most cultures in ancient times honored the graves where their revered ancestors were buried. So Sarah's grave is also honored. A whole chapter (Genesis 23) is devoted to Sarah's place of burial. The final resting place for Sarah, in the sacred grove of Mamre was carefully chosen. It was close to the area where Sarah had spent most of her life. In negotiating for this particular piece of land, Abraham made it clear that it was for Sarah.

There is little question that Sarah was held in high esteem by her husband Abraham. She was a matriarch of authority and position. Abraham asked favors of her. He followed her wishes and desires. This great devotion for Sarah is carried through to the end of her life in the carefully selected and personally owned cemetery.

This beautiful story of Sarah shows God's concern for all people. It demonstrates God's promises in action. Sarah and Abraham lived lives based on these promises — promises moving toward fulfillment. Their trust in these promises was put to many severe tests, and out of these tests of life came the father and mother of a great people. At times they were close to despair, but their greatness consisted in the fact that God called them and through them and their lives, God continues to call and save us.

Here in God's promises to Sarah and Abraham we have the rebellion of humanity being answered. God doesn't give up on his people. This gracious, saving love is to grow with the centuries and comes to fulfillment when the "Word became flesh and lived among us . . . full of grace and truth." (John 1:14)

So we see in this powerful story the faithfulness of God and the power of God's promises. Faith in these promises made a difference! Back to the theme that is holding these sermons together — Sarah and Abraham did not stay the way they were!

We don't have to stay locked into old stereotypes concerning women. One of my favorite stories coming out of the equality movement for women is this one: "Adam and Eve got thrown out of the garden and Eve had to enter the job market. The next big break for women was in 1920 when they got to vote."

The time is long overdue in recognizing that the daughters of God are equal and as important as the sons of God. A concern for church and government is what has been called "The Feminization of Poverty." The growth of poverty among women and children has reached alarming proportions. Two out of three poor adults are women. According to the study by the President's National Advisory Council on Economic Opportunity, by the year 2000 the American poor will consist almost exclusively of women and their children.

Surely another important area for equal recognition is using inclusive, non-sexist language. Some of us don't like the notion but language does reflect our attitude toward women. Our language needs to be subordinate here and not women! Religious bodies are beginning to recognize this by establishing inclusive language policies. One fears that the attempts to trivialize the importance of these changes only show the depth of the problem. But it is important and necessary to create a language that recognizes the dignity and equality of all people. We don't have to stay the way we are!

We remember that "in Christ Jesus neither circumcision nor uncircumcision counts for anything; the only thing that counts is faith working through love." (Galatians 5:6)

We remember in Christian baptism, all receive the gift of love and forgiveness. All receive the power of regeneration and all receive the call to discipleship. Baptism makes no distinctions according to gender, race or class. Hear again the great freedom promise by the apostle Paul:

> *"As many of you as were baptized into Christ have clothed yourselves with Christ. There is no longer Jew or Greek, there is no longer slave or free, there is no longer male and female; for all of you are one in Christ Jesus. And if you belong to Christ, then you are Abraham's offspring, heirs according to the promise."* (Galatians 3:27-28)

---

[1]Savine J. Teubal, *Sarah The Priestess, The First Matriarch of Genesis,* Swallow Press, 1984 and J. H. Otwell, *And Sarah Laughed: The Status of Women in the Old Testament,* Westminster Press, 1977. The above books have been helpful to the author.

[2]Frederick Buechner, *Telling The Truth, The Gospel As Tragedy, Comedy and Fairy Tale,* Harper and Row, 1977, pp. 49-50.

Whatever Happened To Sanctification?

Let Us Pray: Almighty and Merciful God, help us to find our lives by offering them to you. Grant us wisdom to understand your will and the energy to bring your will into our daily lives. Amen.

It has been said that the gospel of Jesus Christ has two sides: ''a believing and a behaving side!'' Followers of Christ are not only invited to be redeemed, but also to be responsible. The Christian faith is not only a way of believing, but a way of living. Years ago, I heard Dr. Alvin Rogness, long-time mentor and teacher in the church, say these words, ''There are no conditions to God's grace. God's grace is free. It is absolutely unconditional, but there are consequences!''

When two Lutheran denominations merged into a new church (ELCA) I supported the new merging church and am happy to be part of it. But once again, in this merging process, there was much discussion, debate and some division over dogma and doctrine. Once again I heard some of the same debates I heard years ago.

Permit a personal example. I have been in public ministry for over 30 years. During those years I have been questioned, sometimes grilled as to whether or not I believed in: a) the infallible, inerrant authority of the Bible, b) a real Jonah who

29

was swallowed by a real fish, c) the Virgin Birth, d) the resurrection of Jesus Christ. Any number of times I have faced the question of "being born again."

Only once in my entire career as an ordained minister of the church, have I ever been questioned as to my lifestyle. I have a letter in my file (grown more precious over the years) that took me to task for supporting and promoting a church remodeling program when there were so many hungry people in the world. The closing shot in that letter was the opinion that pastors who had more than two suits in their closets — were hustlers!

To the best of my recollection (one tends to remember those events!) that has been the only time for that kind of uncomfortable confrontation. Nobody has ever asked me why we need two cars; two bathrooms; two television sets. Nobody has ever asked me why the garage sales to get rid of things so we have room for more things. Nobody has ever asked me how much of our income we give away.

I believe all the above are relevant questions. They reveal not only what I profess to believe, but how I live out what I believe. Of course, it takes no genius to understand why those questions are hardly ever asked. We have a kind of unspoken, secret agreement, you and I. You don't ask me those kinds of questions and I won't ask them of you. It's much safer for us to argue and debate about how we believe the Bible. Whether or not I am following the will of God is a private matter and none of your business. I would like most Christians to put in neutral gear (at least for a time) all debate and controversy over doctrinal issues and into high gear what it means in our time to love our neighbor.

That is the direction of this sermon, under the question: "Whatever happened to sanctification?" Many of us Christians know that we are justified by God — that our sins are forgiven. But some of us are not so good at the follow-through-question: "justified for what?" The answer to that question gets us into the territory of sanctification which has to do with how we practice what we say we believe. Simply stated: "sanctification is the call to holy living."

Our Old Testament text for this Sunday can give us some guidance on this issue. We have in front of us this morning the Exodus description of the 10 commandments. In the book of Deuteronomy (Deuteronomy 5:6-21) we have a similar description of this momentous event. Don't be troubled if the numbering system by which you memorized the commandments is different than our text. Various Christian denominations have numbered the commandments differently, depending on how they combined or divided the biblical texts. The commandments, however, remain the same.

First of all, let us be reminded, that nowhere in the Bible do we find the faintest hint that we do not have to take the commandments of God seriously. Nor do we find anything in our theology that would suggest we do not have to take the commandments of God seriously. Over half of Luther's Large Catechism is devoted to the 10 commandments. Luther certainly knew, believed, taught and preached that Christians are not saved by the laws of God. Why then, all this attention to these laws? Because God's commandments are given to us out of God's love and they become the means of expressing that love to our neighbors. The commandments are not given to create more misery and unhappiness in our lives. Rather they come with the promise to make our lives more meaningful, abundant and satisfying. So it is important to remember that the commandments of God have not been repealed — they are still in force. But it is even more important to know and believe that God's commandments are not a burden.

There used to be a television show where Maude says to Walter, "God will get you for that, Walter!" We laugh, but that kind of popular religion goes deeper than many of us want to admit. We seem to be born with the attitude or feeling that our God is against us and somehow needs to be bought off. This means that if we don't obey God's commandments, God will get even. So it is very important to know, to be reminded, to believe that the commandments of God came to the people of Israel from a God who was for, not against, them. If you remember nothing else from this sermon remember how God introduces the commandments, "I am the Lord your God, who brought you out of the land of Egypt, out of the house of bondage." (Exodus 20:2) God has saved the people of Israel. They have been redeemed from slavery in Egypt. It is in this context that God establishes the covenant with the people of God.

Remember, the Old Testament (Covenant) primarily saw the acts of God as "acts of deliverance." It is this great act of deliverance from government oppression which gave shape and content to the faith of the people of God. This Exodus event is the decisive event in their history. From this day onward, Israel belonged to God.

So the giving of the commandments provided the climax of the great story of the people of God, fleeing from the government of Egypt, wandering in the wilderness, and then the mountain experience at Sinai. The commandments of God is the charter, the content of the covenant obligation because "God's people were not intended to be a crowd but a community, bound to God and to one another by a covenant bond."[1]

But again, remember that the commandments are not orders sent down from on high by some distant and unfeeling commander. Rather the commandments come out of a caring, loving relationship. The commandments of God are given to help and guide us in the tough business of living.

Take the commandment: "You shall not bear false witness against your neighbor." This has to do with lying. We can get into all kinds of games as to what is a lie. Most of us are guilty of some social lies about how we feel or how we evaluate another's appearance. Here, in love, we may fudge on the truth a bit. Bearing false witness has to do with more important issues than these. It has to do with public and political lying: lying to protect our job or our reputation, lying to get ahead by ruining the reputation of another, lying to sell goods, lying to make a profit, lying to get re-elected, lying about our income to the IRS, lying to make our country look good, lying under the excuse of national security.

These kinds of lies are never trivial. They erode away the foundation of truth which is a basic ingredient for any successful, enduring civilization. Our century has been called the century of the "big lie." George Forell has written, "Lying is a cancer destroying the connective tissues of society."[2] When truth becomes whatever people in power say it is, then slowly but surely, trust is replaced by cynicism, and loyalty is for sale to the highest bidder.

In a strong, courageous book on Jesus' Sermon on the Mount titled *Into the Darkness,* Gene Davenport shares these thoughts about this commandment:

> *"Perhaps the most influential expression of language's bondage to the Darkness in Western society today live in a society characterized by duplicity. One of the primary characteristics of the Powers of Darkness, lying has been elevated to the rank of heroic morality by the government and to the status of art in ordinary commerce."*[3]

Claude Lewis, a columnist for the *Philadelphia Inquirer*, wrote these words: "It is 1989 and nothing's changed. We have lived this long in America to learn that if anything at all has been eternally established it is that the truth is what government says it is."

He concludes his strong article with this strong indictment: "National security is a misnomer in politics . . . the two most abused words in modern politics when placed side by side are 'national' and 'security.' In the mouths of presidents and politicians the words are used to hide a multitude of sins."[4]

How can one have any kind of meaningful relationship with people who do not tell the truth? There is no way for useful communication with lying people. Families experience turmoil and alienation when members are no longer truthful with one another. Healthy, loving relationships between husband and wife require honesty and truthfulness. This commandment by God is for our well being. Life becomes hell when the lie becomes a way of life. Therefore, sanctified Christians do not lie. We are champions for the truth. We don't stand still for governments who lie. We speak up when gossip is used to hurt people. We don't tolerate racist jokes. This is obedience to the eighth commandment. This is living the sanctified life.

The sixth commandment: "Thou shalt not commit adultery" (Exodus 20:14) receives much attention in our time, but obedience to it is another question. Some are so obsessed with sex that they want to make it the focus of all sin. In recent years we have had popular television evangelists proclaiming the gospel of Jesus Christ while living in luxurious surroundings and following a materialistic lifestyle far removed from the example of Christ. Yet this kind of gracious living seemed to enhance their popularity. Only when some of them got caught violating the sixth commandment, did some of their adoring public turn on them. One gets the impression that people are not immoral even though they lie, steal, covet or cheat their neighbor, as long as they abstain from illicit sex.

For Christians sex is a gift from God. Sex is a part of God's created order. The fact that women and men are sexually attracted to each other makes life richer, more exciting and beautiful. But to live for sex as to live for food is to make it into an idol. When sex becomes an idol, like all idols, it destroys human relationships, rather than enhancing them.

Again quoting George Forell, "Trivializing sexuality, making it a means of selling merchandise, or merely passing time, undermines and reveals the sickness of our society. It is not the cause of our difficulties, but it is an obvious and powerful symptom. Sex is not ruining our society; idolatry, our empty life without God is ruining sex ...."[5]

Which brings us back to the first commandment: "I am the Lord your God, who brought you out of the land of Egypt, out of the house of bondage. You shall have no other gods before me." (Exodus 20:2-3) It is this commandment which raises the basic question: "Where is the center of my life?" Maybe the center of my life is ambition and I am going to do whatever is necessary to get ahead — lie, if that is necessary.

Or maybe our idol is sex and we become obsessed with quantity rather than quality and as a result become a person who loves nobody, least of all himself or herself.

In the commandments, God is telling us that we don't have to live that way. The commandments from a loving God are a description of what God can make out of our lives. We don't have to stay the way we are. God's commandments are not a burden but a blessing. Justification and sanctification belong together.

In the season of Lent, we see once again the cross of Christ revealing the great loving heart of God. It is because of the cross that the apostle Paul could say, "Do not be conformed to this world but be transformed . . . ." (Romans 12:2) This is sanctified living. Amen.

---

[1]Bernhard W. Anderson, *Understanding the Old Testament,* (Englewood Cliffs, Prentice-Hall, Inc. 1957) p. 53.

[2]Useful to me in this sermon on the commandments was a 12-part series on the commandments appearing in the *Lutheran Standard* (1982) by George W. Forell, Carver Distinguished Professor of Religion at the University of Iowa, Iowa City.

[3]Gene Davenport, *Into the Darkness*, (Nashville, Abingdon Press, 1988), p. 72.

[4]Claude Lewis, " 'National Security' hides nation's sins," *The Des Moines Register*, Summer, 1989.

[5]*Ibid,* George W. Forell.

Lift High
The Cross

Last Sunday we left the people of Israel at Mount Sinai where they had received the commandments of God. They spent about a year at this holy mountain. (They arrived at Sinai in Exodus 19:1; they did not break camp until Numbers 10:11.) In our text for today, they are on the move again through the trackless wilderness. Their wilderness wanderings were the best and the worst of times for these chosen ones of God. On the one hand it was the time when God and the people were on close and intimate terms. God delivered them from Egypt. Looking back on this decisive moment in their history, the people of God made this memorable confession:

And you shall make response before the Lord your God, "A wandering Aramean was my father; and he went down into Egypt and sojourned there, few in number; and there he became a nation, great, mighty, and populous. And the Egyptians treated us harshly, and afflicted us, and laid upon us hard bondage. Then we cried to the Lord the God of our fathers, and the Lord heard our voice, and saw our affliction, our toil, and our oppression; and the Lord brought us out of Egypt with a mighty hand and an outstretched arm, with great terror, with signs and wonders . . . ." (Deuteronomy 26:5-8)

37

So the chosen ones experienced God's great care and attention, through the Exodus from Egypt to the holy mountain of Sinai where they received guidance for obedience and service. God did not supply all their wants, but God saw to all their physical and spiritual needs — at a time when they were helpless and had nowhere to turn.

But it was also the worst of times. Wilderness wandering, whining and complaining went together. But what is really surprising in all this grumbling is the disgusting regularity with which the Israelites wanted to return to the security of making bricks out of straw under the orders of the oppressive government of Egypt. It seems that the security of slavery was more important than the freedom of the wilderness. (The Bible does not read like some romance story. It is uncomfortably and candidly honest!)

So in our story today, "they were on the road again," avoiding the enemy territory of Edom, grumbling and impatient as usual. They were wearing out and so was their leader, Moses. Moses was probably wondering why he ever left the flesh pots of Egypt or the quiet, tranquil life of a shepherd herding his father-in-law's sheep. Again and again Moses had learned that it is a lot easier to deal with woolly sheep than woolly people. They accused him of inept leadership when they ran short of water. He continued to get it when they ran short of food. He was a leader who was also caught in the middle. If he wasn't busy convincing his people that God had really called him, he was busy arguing with God that the people were worth calling.

Once again Moses heard the familiar lament, "Why did you bring us out of Egypt to die in this desert, where there is no food or water? We can't stand any more of this miserable food." Their attitude reminds me a bit of my student days at college and our consistent complaining about the miserable, tasteless, starchy food we were being served in the cafeteria. But nobody took our complaining too seriously!

The children of Israel were not so fortunate. God heard and God acted and now we have the strange story of the snakes.

"Then the Lord sent poisonous snakes among the people and many Israelites were bitten and died." This Old Testament story is a difficult one for our modern, scientific ears. God's people were certainly behaving in an obnoxious fashion, but the punishment seems a bit severe. Does God really turn rattlesnakes loose among people? Can one be healed simply by looking at the bronze or copper image of a snake that is mounted on a pole? That sounds like magical hocus-pocus, a voodoo kind of healing that believers in God are supposed to avoid. Well, we can make the technical point that God sent the snakes, but it was the people who stepped on them! It also seems clear that it was God and not the snakes that caused the healing.

Perhaps it might be of additional help to learn that snakes have a rather interesting, if ambiguous religious history. The snake was cursed by God to forever crawl in the dust for its role in the sin of Adam and Eve. Here in our story the snake is elevated on a pole for healing purposes. We know that even today, the image of the serpent is the healing symbol for our medical profession. We still have snake cults among some religious people in Appalachia who handle the poisonous reptiles as a sign of their strong faith in God.

There is some evidence that there was a snake cult operating among the people of Israel. It was probably the "physical healing" dimension of their faith. The Bible tells us of this kind of snake worship in the temple of Jerusalem during the reign of King Hezekiah. (2 Kings 18:4) Apparently, it was getting out of hand, because the good king had the image destroyed.

Archeologists have uncovered bronze images of snakes in an abandoned copper mine that could have been the location of this particular crisis, but this is a highly speculative conclusion.

We are dealing here with a lot of tangled history that will probably never be completely unraveled. But there is considerable evidence that the appearance of snakes in this wilderness crisis was something more than just a coincidence, and something more than voodoo magic at the hands of an unseeing and uncaring God.

Now you have probably heard more about snakes than you wanted to. But down through history to the present time, snakes continue to exert both their frightening and fascinating power. In our gospel reading for today, we have the surprising connection between the snake on the pole and the Son of God on the cross. If nothing else, John in his gospel makes clear the primary point, and that is that God provided the means of healing after the people had repented.

That is what happened in our Old Testament story. Once the people of God discovered how awful it was to live with snakes, they came to their senses again and confessed to Moses, "We have sinned for we have spoken against the Lord and against you; pray to the Lord, that he take away the serpents from us." Living with snakes proved to be no picnic! It prompted an attitudinal change. It doesn't always work that way. Sometimes increased suffering produces even greater bitterness and alienation. Here, however, it called forth the spirit of repentance and confession.

It is important to note that the prayers of the Israelites were not answered in the way they requested. The snakes were not removed. Instead the image of a snake was created out of bronze, lifted upon a pole and all who were bitten and then looked upon this image would survive. But of all creatures of God that could have been lifted up — a snake! A snake is lifted up to be the sign of healing, of salvation! That is very strange to us. It strikes us as just a bit more than unusual. Lift high the snake! To hear it said that way is offensive to our ears. It sounds crude and awful. A teenager would describe it as "gross."

But in his gospel, John takes this "gross" incident and tells us, "And as Moses lifted up the serpent in the wilderness, so much the Son of man be lifted up, that whoever believes in him may have eternal life." (John 3:14-15)

Undoubtedly this connection between the Old and New Testaments is the most important insight in our Biblical readings for this Sunday. In the Old Testament, the snake is lifted up. In the New Testament, Christ is lifted up.

Lift high the cross! There is something gross about that too. It's just that we have put so much gold plating around it and hung it around so many necks as decoration that it no longer looks or sounds offensive. I suspect this is one of the reasons the empty cross has replaced the crucifix in so many of our churches. We don't want to see or even be reminded of the suffering and dying Christ who was nailed to it. But it was a lowly Jewish carpenter who was executed on such a cross as a common criminal. Yes, the chief symbol of our church today, the cross, was the electric chair of the first century.

So the great missionary Paul saw the cross as a "scandal to Jews and folly to the Gentiles" because it was hard for them to accept a suffering redeemer, a wounded healer. They and we are more comfortable with a God of power and majesty, but what we have is a carpenter's son from the little town of Nazareth — one who came humble and meek and whose life ended high upon the cursed tree.

Yes, the story in front of us this morning is strange to our ears, but strange or not, our story continues to reveal a God who is faithfully consistent. In the 40 years of wandering in the wilderness, through all the moaning and complaining of the called ones, God remained faithful to the agreement (promise) that was made with them.

For the children of Israel the wilderness was that time between God's deliverance from Egypt and their entry into the promised land. In our life, the wilderness is that time between the dying and rising of Christ and when Christ comes again. So we are now on our wilderness journey. We live in the in-between-time. In our wilderness trip, we too have our "snakes" with which to contend — snakes that poison our lives. We also do our share of groaning and complaining. Yes, we live in our wilderness too, only the geography is different.

So lift high the cross! Look upon this cross and see there the sign of our healing, the sign of our salvation. Among other things, the cross is the great symbol of God's continuing faithfulness to us. This God who refused to give up on the Israelites of old, will not give up on the baptized ones of the present.

41

Yes, lift high the cross! Let it remind us that our God knows that living can be hard and our suffering can be great. Our God in Christ has experienced wilderness living. God has appreciation and understanding of our feeble attempts to live and love in a wilderness full of snakes.

So lift high the cross! The uplifted cross proclaims to us that God's love for us is not based upon our successes, our social standing, our bank account, our prestige — not even on our grade averages at school. The cross is and remains the symbol of God's great and unconditional love for us.

Lift high the cross! See there your Redeemer and know "that whoever believes in him should not perish, but have eternal life."

Lift high the cross. Amen.

The Right
Spirit Within Us . . .

Today, in our Old Testament journey to Easter, we make a significant adjustment both in time, geography and attitude. We are at that momentous year of 587 B.C. (or slightly beyond) when the country of Judah is no more. The beautiful temple, built in the great days of King Solomon is no more. This holy, awesome temple has been sacked and its priceless art treasures carried off to the wicked country of Babylon. The monarchy, reaching back to the golden days of King David is no more. The holy city of Jerusalem is in ruins. God's people have become God's refugees.

Jeremiah was prophet before, during and after these dreadful and unbelievable events. He was the pastor/preacher/prophet during this twilight time of his people. One hundred or so years earlier, the Northern Kingdom of Israel had fallen and was no more. Now the Southern Kingdom of Judah was on the verge of collapse. Jeremiah was called a traitor because he preached this bad news. His government, like most governments, wanted a more positive message. News of "doom and gloom" was bad for the economy and for re-election. This was true because most people didn't want to hear such messages either. The people of God had grown so used to "God talk" that there was no question that God was on their side.

The uncomfortable insights of Old Testament scholar, Walter Brueggemann, are helpful at this point:

> *"They are fascinated with statistics. They are skilled at press conferences. They believe their own propaganda. They imagine that God loves rather than judges, that the Babylonian threat will soon disappear, (cf. Jeremiah 28:2-4) that the economy is almost back to normal, that Judean values will somehow survive, that religion needs to be affirmative, that things will hold together if we all hug each other."*

Dr. Brueggeman concludes, "In a word, they believe that grief is treason .... They are into happiness, optimism and well-being."[1]

With that optimistic mind-set, there is little "covenant" concern for the poor and defenseless victims of their time. Covenant living is living with concern and compassion for the community. But God's people were becoming more "individualistic" — more focused on self and personal needs. About the country's growing greedy, selfish spirit, hear Jeremiah's strong words to King Jehoikim, son of the good King Josiah:

> *"Do you think you are a king*
>   *because you compete in cedar?*
> *Did not your father eat and drink*
>   *and do justice and righteousness?*
> *Then it was well with him.*
> *He judged the cause of the poor and needy;*
>   *then it was well.*
> *Is not this to know me? says the Lord.*
> *But you have eyes and heart*
>   *only for dishonest gain,*
>   *for shedding innocent blood,*
>   *and for practicing oppression and violence."*
> (22:15-17)

This is what Jeremiah saw as he watched his country die. By this kind of behavior Israel had defiled and polluted the promised land, turning it into a wilderness where God's name was profaned. By disrespect for God, Israel had made holy land unholy. In Israel's failure to honor God, the covenant God had made with them was broken.

Remember? The covenant business began with Noah and God's promise never again to send judgment via the flood, and the rainbow was the sign. Again, God called Abraham and Sarah to be the father and mother of a people through whom all people would be blessed. This covenant relationship was confirmed and renewed with Moses at Mount Sinai where God gave the 10 commandments.

Jeremiah compares the covenant relationship between God and the people to a marriage relationship between a man and a woman. But Israel was the unfaithful spouse in this relationship. So Jeremiah preached:

> "They have turned back to the iniquities of their forefathers, who refused to hear my words; they have gone after other gods to serve them; the house of Judah have broken my covenant which I made with their fathers."
> (11:10)

These iniquities brought an end to a way of life that would never return.

Jeremiah's life and message raises the uncomfortable question: When is treason patriotism, and when is patriotism treason? We seem to live in a time when any criticism of our country is regarded as unpatriotic. Yet, the sermons of the Old Testament prophets were directed primarily toward the sins of their own country. They seemed to be much more suspicious of patriotic fervor than we are inclined to be. I think about Jeremiah and the flag controversy in our country. I also think about how popular and important the swastika flag was for Germany 50 years ago. In any public event, church or secular, this national symbol was in prominent display. Does not history tell us that flag worship and idolatry are much more dangerous than flag desecration? Jeremiah's example is a useful one when we make judgments about loyalty and patriotism. By many of his people, he was looked upon as a traitor and a failure. But history judges him differently.

Jeremiah was a prophet called by God to preach an unpopular but realistic word to a people who did not want to hear it. Yet his word was not only one of warning, but also one of hope, for into this somber picture of hopelessness came these now familiar comforting words of hope, "Behold, the days are coming."

Many biblical scholars believe that in this prophecy, Jeremiah's thinking and preaching reaches its climax. It is regarded by many as one of the mountain peaks of the Old Testament. It is quoted extensively in the Book of Hebrews and we recall its use in the memorable words by Jesus in the institution of the holy supper — "This cup is the new covenant in my blood." (Luke 22:20) Little wonder that this memorable text is described as "the gospel before the gospel."

Jeremiah looked to a new future and to a new time beyond the lost world. This prophet, who had such true, but tough words about judgment, could also speak true and loving words of hope, "Behold, the days are coming ..."

But what is coming? What is this word of hope?

It is the hope of a "right spirit within us." This is the new word that Jeremiah brought the despondent exiles. He did not call for renewed repentance. Instead, he spoke a word of radical grace, from the heart of God:

> *Thus says the Lord of hosts, the God of Israel: "The days are surely coming ... I will put my law within them, and I will write it on their hearts; and I will be their God, and they shall be my people." (31:31ff)*

The preacher Ezekiel, a younger contemporary of Jeremiah, preached the same promise of hope in these words:

> *"A new heart I will give you, and a new spirit I will put within you; and I will take out of your flesh the heart of stone and give you a heart of flesh." (36:2)*

46

"Circumcision of the heart" is what is needed. The spiritual life must be from the inside out. Jeremiah was on the threshold of seeing the need for inward conversion and being born anew. This was God's promise to the people of God. No longer was the law to be just a code regulating outward behavior. Under the new covenant (agreement) God's spirit was to be working inside of us.

One cannot presume that Jeremiah knew how God was going to create this "right spirit within us." But Christians looking back, see the cross of Christ as the fulfillment of God's promise. In today's gospel we hear the Son of God say, "My hour has come ... and when I am lifted up from the earth (that is crucified), I will draw all people to myself." (John 12:32)

Jesus sees his death, for all people — for you and me. Here is the new day, the new hope God promised and Jeremiah looked forward to. Here is power for this new spirit within us. It is created not by rules but by love that has died for me. The new covenant is not another law to be obeyed to make one's self righteous and often times self-righteous. Instead, sinners will be filled from within to do what is right, filled with desire to do God's will.

This transformation comes about in grateful response to what a forgiving God has done for us. This is the drawing power of the cross. Because of this event, we can change, we don't have to stay the way we are. The love of God revealed on the cross empowers us to respond in love. In this relationship there is true desire to do that which is pleasing to God.

"Behold, the days are coming ... when the law will be written in the heart." Christians see this promise of hope being fulfilled through the death and resurrection of Jesus Christ.

But one is fearful that this good news produces just a big yawn! After all, what else is new? We are not living in exile. We are not homesick for home.

Or are we? Or should we be?

Maybe our "way of living" is located in a "foreign land" and we know it not. Who are the "Jewish prophets" of our time — the prophets who are unpatriotic, rejected and very unpopular? Do we pay any attention to them? Is Jesus a threat to us? To our way of living? He was a threat in his day and was crucified because of it.

If life "can't get no better than this" what's the point of a hope-filled promise? Unless, we too, like Israelites of old have put on the rose-colored glasses and have become willing victims of deception.

Again, the helpful insights of Brueggemann, whom I believe is one of the prophets of our time:

> *"I believe that we are in a season of transition, when we are watching the collapse of the world as we have known it. ... The news is that God enters the broken ... In God's attentive pain, healing happens. Newness comes. Possibilities are presented ..."*[2]

I agree with Brueggemann's diagnosis. I think this country is in a transition time. "Behold, the days are coming ..." In store for us could be "days" of hurting and homesickness. But the promise of newness and hope is also there. One of the important lessons through our Lenten journey is that God remains faithful to the covenant made with us.

In the New Covenant, the dying-rising-life power of God's Son is shared with the followers of God. Jesus tells us, "Where I am, there shall my servant be also." (John 12:26) Here is the answer to a life homesick for home. Here is the answer to wilderness living. Here is the answer to a life that has become an existence. Here is the key that opens the door to purposeful and meaningful living. It is not where I breathe that I live, but where I love that I really live. Selfishness is the end of life while sacrifice is the salvation of life. The new heart, the new creation brought into fulfillment by our Lord's dying and rising provides the motivation for a dying life — a life that is hope-filled life. That is life with the right spirit within us. That is life with true joy because it is a life that is being used up for others.

No, our lives are not there, but God's promise is and remains — "Behold the day is coming . . ." We continue to pray with the psalmist:

"O God close your eyes to my sins
and wipe out all my evil.
Create a pure heart in me, O God
and put a new and right spirit in me." (Psalm 51)

---

[1]Walter Brueggemann, *Hopeful Imagination,* Fortress, 1986, p. 42. This is an excellent book. I am indebted to Dr. Brueggemann for some of the thoughts and ideas for these sermons dealing with God's people in exile.

[2]*Ibid,* pp. 46-74.

Passion Sunday
Isaiah 50:4-9a

Courageous Preaching

Suppose reliable word came that within hours this area of the country would be attacked by enemy missiles. Orders from the military broadcast over the emergency stations tell us to evacuate our town and literally run for our lives.

Perhaps we would quickly plan some strategy of escape, maybe with some close friends and relatives. Or we might hold a hurried congregational meeting and decide to leave in some sort of protective caravan. No matter what our specific response, all of a sudden we would experience what it is like to become a homeless people. Suddenly, without warning, we are part of that vast number of refugees whose chief goal becomes survival.

We soon discover that nobody wants us. Everywhere we run into negative attitudes: "We have enough economic problems and unemployment the way it is. We don't need you people adding to it. Move on — we don't have room for you here." We keep on the move, getting farther and farther from home. Night after night we look into the frightened eyes of our children who ask, "Where are we going now? Why can't we go home?"

It so happens that we are among the few fortunate refugees. A Moslem country opens its doors to us and we are permitted to enter and settle down the best we can. So we are no longer refugees. Now we are exiles, learning how to start over in a foreign land. It is hard! We are accepted but with great suspicion. In addition we have the language problem. Their style of life and religious practices are strange to us and vice versa. We live "frightened" most of the time. We don't want to run any risks which might antagonize our hosts. At home we had everything. Here we have next to nothing. Not even a church to worship in. We are homesick for home and the way things used to be.

We cry:

> *"It is nothing to you, all you who pass by*
> *Look and see if there is any sorrow like my sorrow*
>   *which was brought upon me.*
> *Which the Lord inflicted*
>   *on the day of his fierce anger ...*
> *My eyes are spent with weeping;*
>   *my soul is in tumult;*
> *My heart is poured out in grief ... "*
> (Lamentations, chapters 1 and 2)

But we can't go home. Though discouraged, depressed and oppressed, we have to make the best of it. We have our families to take care of. So we make do. We get what jobs we can. We struggle to learn the language. We work at our trades and use our skills.

Over the years we begin to put down roots in this foreign land and memory of home begins to fade. A generation passes. The adjusting, assimilating and adapting continues. There are many inter-marriages. It is even getting hard to tell the Moslems from the Christians. It seems now, that the only time we hear anything about home is in our worship service. The preachers keep telling us stories about how things used to be and that the day will come when we will return home. But we really don't believe them. We have heard these promises so many times before. Besides, our hosts aren't so bad once you get to know them. We are safe. We aren't hungry anymore.

So the memory of home is gradually replaced by an eroding faith and changing values.

Last Sunday's text spoke about the people of God at the most discouraging time of their history — becoming displaced persons in the heathen country of Babylon. They were a sad, homesick group of people and Jeremiah was their preacher who in their despair, reminded them of the hope-filled promises of God.

In our Old Testament lesson for today, we are deeper into the Babylonian exile. But no longer is Babylon the only super power around. The Persian empire is on the rise and Babylon is on the verge of collapse. As Jeremiah saw Nebuchadnezzar as an agent of God's judgment, so the new prophet on the scene, Isaiah, sees Persia under the rule of Cyrus, as an agent of God's restoration.

The prophet in our text for today, proclaims to the people of God living in exile, the hope of returning home. It is not clear whether it is the prophet or one of his disciples who is preaching, but this is the word that is preached, "The Lord God has given me the tongue of those who are taught, that I may know how to sustain with a word him that is weary."

The book of Isaiah, perhaps as no other book in the Bible, stresses the importance and power of God's word. We read these familiar words, "The grass withers, the flower fades; but the word of our God will stand forever." Again these words in that great reassuring promise:

> "For as the rain and the snow come down
>   from heaven,
> and return not thither but water the
>   earth,
> making it bring forth and sprout,
>   giving seed to the sower and bread
> to the eater,
>   so shall my word be that goes forth
> from my mouth;
>   it shall not return to me empty,

but it shall accomplish that which I
    purpose,
and prosper in the thing for which I
    sent it." (Isaiah 55:10-11)

"Faith comes by hearing" the apostle Paul reminded Roman Christians many centuries later. In our text the preacher strives to revive hope in the weary and frustrated exiles through the gift of words. In an intensely personal (in this short passage the preacher mentions: cheeks, beard, face, tongue, ear and back!) and in poetic fashion, words are put together to remind a downhearted people of their heritage.

We take note that this particular preacher speaks as one who has first been spoken to. We read:

"Morning by morning he wakens,
    he wakens my ear
    to hear as those who are taught.
The Lord God has opened my ear,
    and I was not rebellious,
    I turned not backward." (50:5-6)

It has been suggested that "listening" is the greatest service that Christians can give to other people.

Sometimes preachers forget that listening can be a greater service than speaking, because many people are looking for an ear rather than a mouth. Dietrich Bonhoeffer, the German Christian martyr, whose execution anniversary is April 9, 1945, said these words about the importance of listening:

"The first service that one owes to others in the fellowship is listening to them ... They (clergy) forget that listening can be a greater service than speaking ... Anyone who thinks that his time is too valuable to spend keeping quiet will eventually have no time for God ... We should listen with the ears of God that we may speak the Word of God."[1]

Bonhoeffer believed that inspired listening and speaking went together. The preacher in our text listened. We are told that he listened with an "open ear." This means he could hear something different without closing his mind to it. Our preacher was an open-minded speaker and listener. But many of his listeners were not so like-minded! They did not like what they heard. Somewhere I read the story about the person who did not like the pastor's preaching. The minute the pastor began preaching, he picked up his newspaper and began to read. (Don't you get any ideas!)

One thing could be said for the preacher in our text. He obviously didn't bore people or put them to sleep with the sermon. We are told that the listeners, at least at times, became quite violent and volatile; "I gave my back to the smiters, and my cheeks to those who pulled out the beard; I hid not my face from shame and spitting." Such was the severe reaction this servant of God experienced as he demonstrated that he was not afraid to be unpopular. Sometimes memories of home are very painful.

So our text gives emphasis to the importance and need of courageous preaching. It has been said that the greatest sin in the church today has become the sin of "hurting someone's feelings." Of course, preachers should not measure their success by the number of people they make unhappy or angry. But neither should preachers be bribed with popularity, for we are not called to please our customers. Grady Davis, a great teacher of preachers a generation ago, wrote these words: "The gospel is meant for everybody, but it cannot be what everybody would like it to be. The preacher is called to create taste, not to satisfy tastes."[2]

One of the reasons people sleep through our sermons is because too many of them are so bland and safe. If at times we do take a stand on a controversial issue, we tend to fog it up in abstract language so that our listeners can interpret it the way they want to. So the theologian's flower has been called the "hedge" and wise old Joe Sittler talked about coming down on an issue "with both feet planted in mid-air!"

Yes, strong sermons will evoke disagreement, but I believe there remains in our congregations a deep hunger for more plain talk from the pulpit. Our people are getting weary of words that distort and conceal.

Some of the reasons for the strong sermon reaction in our text is that the exiled people had adapted, adjusted and assimilated in their new environment. They no longer felt like "exiles." Where Jeremiah preached to a homesick people, Isaiah preached to a people in danger of forgetting home. Exile living not only caused despair, it also created amnesia. The people of God became comfortable living in exile, and comfort dulled their memory of home. They were getting tired and angry about the old stories and promises of home. Some probably doubted whether or not the preachers knew what they were talking about, for it seems that preachers are always making those impractical, grandiose promises for God.

So the threat of Babylon changed into the temptation of Babylon. Babylon became home. It seemed to be one of those tough truths that go with living: When we ignore our history, we make an idol out of the present and we booby-trap the future. We live only for today. We forget we are the caretakers of God's word and promises. We sabotage the future and the generations who will follow us. Exile living becomes more than just a matter of geography. It can also bring with it the erosion of memory and faith.[3] Time and time again the chosen people of God were reminded of this danger:

> *"Take heed lest you forget the Lord your God . . . lest, when you have eaten and are full, and have built goodly houses and live in them, and when your herds and flocks multiply, and your silver and gold is multiplied, then your heart be lifted up, and you forget the Lord your God, who brought you out of the land of Egypt, out of the house of bondage."* (Deuteronomy 8:11-15)

Multiplication of things and amnesia seem to go together. Comfort also encourages amnesia. Security encourages amnesia. Many of the people of God adjusted well in their new country. They were becoming satisfied in their new home. They did not want to think about packing up, making the long journey back to their home land and starting all over again.

One wonders if Christians in this country do not face a similar problem. No, we don't live in a foreign land ala my introductory story. But in our day there are more subtle and dangerous kinds of captivity. In his day Martin Luther talked about the "Babylonian captivity of the Roman Catholic Church." Is it possible that the Christian Church in our country is captive to the American way of life?" A good student of the Old Testament as well as of American living thinks so. Dr. Brueggemann writes:

> *"We may observe how very easily American Christianity comes to identify with Western capitalism, the free market system, and the values that grow from there. Or, more acutely, how easily we are enveloped into consumer militarism, which roughly characterizes the main value tendency of American society. Consumerism is the seduction that getting, having and using is the main mode of humanness . . . The values of consumerism as they are personally appropriated tend to an intense narcissism and an expectation of self-gratification."*[4]

There is little question that there is an erosion of faith going on in our time. Unchurched (dechurched might be a more accurate description) America numbers 90 million and growing. Does not our own backyard represent one of the largest and most challenging mission fields for the church? There are probably many reasons for this growing disenchantment with the church (I suspect that many people are simply bored with us!) but our growing lust for comfort and pleasure seems to be a major contributing factor to our growing amnesia. Martin Marty tells us that "the God killers today are not Marx, Freud and Darwin . . . but high rise apartments, long weekends and mobility." There is little question that the "pull of the world," (getting/having/using) is a powerful and tempting force in our day. It is easy for us to forget that "here we have no lasting city, but seek the city which is to come.'' (Hebrews 13:14)

The central task of the last half of the book of Isaiah is to persuade the people of God that even after two generations, Babylon is still not their home! Yes, to remind them that their exile from their homeland did not mean exile from their God. God's compassion had taken the form of judgment, but it was not nullified. God was not defeated. God's promises for them were still valid.

We, who may be in danger of being seduced by the power of the world, need to hear that God's word is more powerful than any country, any ideology, any ism — even consumerism! We do not have to stay captive to our culture. We do not have to stay captive to things.

Our source of strength is not in getting and getting but in the power of the Spirit working through God's word. That is one of the important reasons for attending church. Here is where our memories are refreshed that we do not forget our true home.

The preacher in our text was not discouraged. God had given him the word of hope and it was delivered, even at the expense of ridicule and suffering. Much in the same way, Jesus' suffering was the result of his strong preaching of God's kingdom and his obedient life — even in the face of rejection. It seems that true and courageous prophets never have had an easy time of it. Jesus laments, ''O Jerusalem, Jerusalem, killing the prophets and stoning those who are sent to you!'' Those who tell new truths or remind people of forgotten truths are ''troublers of the faith'' who expose the complacency of the faithful. They are seldom thanked for their pains.

It is not an easy message to hear — that the gospel of Jesus Christ and the world do not always fit well together. Yet, it is one that we need to hear lest the comforts of our exiled living dull the memory of our true home.

We are in the final days of our journey to Easter. Holy Week is an especially fitting symbol to remind us that our identity is with the Suffering Servant and not with the ''make-you-rich-Messiah.'' Obedience and denial can bring suffering. Living our Christian convictions in a time of affluence can bring suffering. That is the way of the cross, but it is also where our true home is. Amen.

---

[1]Dietrich Bonhoeffer, *Life Together,* (New York, Harper and Row, 1954), pp. 97-99.

[2]H. Grady Davis, *Design for Preaching,* Fortress, 1958, p. 7.

[3]Walter Brueggemann, *Hopeful Imagination,* Fortress Press, 1986, p. 42.

[4]*Ibid,* pp. 92-127.

All We Like Sheep
Have Gone Astray

In the middle 1960s, a seminary student interned in a Lutheran congregation in Berlin, Germany. This intern was much interested in the history of World War II, since he was born about the time his father was fighting in Germany. However, he soon discovered that most of the members of that congregation did not want to talk about the war. It was too painful. But one day, an uncle of one of the intern's friends came to see him and shared this personal story.[1]

He was an engineer on the train from Amsterdam to Auschwitz. He was on the run that transported Jews to their death. Most of the Jews carried in these cattle cars were old men, women and children. (Of the six million Jews killed in the Holocaust, one million were children!) At one of the stops on this journey, when they cleaned some of the filth and dead bodies from the cattle cars, the engineer was busy making his inspection of the train. First he heard the voice, then he saw the extended hand of a woman reaching through the boards and crying for water. She told the engineer that her baby was sick, running a high temperature and desperately needed some water.

The engineer was afraid. Yet, he felt compelled by the woman's moving plea. He went to get some water. As he was about to place the small pail of water into the outstretched hand, he felt the stab of cold steel against his neck. He turned ever so slowly and saw the uniform with the bayonet. And then he heard these cold words, "If you want to give her the water, get in the car." What seemed like an eternity, but in reality only a few seconds, the engineer held on to the pail, then dropped it and walked back to his engine.

That is one painful picture that is hard to erase from one's memory. Although I heard this story many years ago, its haunting power remains ever fresh in my mind. If I had been the engineer, what would I have done? Or the woman with the sick baby? Or been the person in uniform? What kind of evil forces these terrible and tragic decisions upon us?

We are nearing the end of our journey to the cross and to Easter. It has been suggested that the cross of Christ marks the end of the "masquerade ball of humanity." At the cross, our masks come off and we see behind our pretty poses and pious disguises.

To encourage us once again to "stand beneath this cross" and contemplate its meaning for our lives, we have the mysterious, yet comforting words of the Suffering Servant written in the book of Isaiah.

These words too, are directed to an evil time — to God's people who are suffering in exile. As we have been hearing these past weeks, it is a time of turmoil and fear. It is also a time when physical misery is compounded by growing doubts about their God who has not or cannot fulfill the promised blessings. The pull and power of Babylon seems so much stronger than the God of Abraham, Isaac and Jacob.

One of the significant, additional burdens of suffering for the imprisoned people in Germany was the growing spirit of hopelessness. In their concentration camps, there was "no light at the end of the tunnel." For all they could see and hear, Hitler's rule would last for 1,000 years. So also the mood and attitude of the people of God living in exile; "I have labored in vain, I have spent my strength for nought, and in vain."

But into this mood of helplessness and hopelessness comes the stirring words of hope from the prophet (or prophets)

Isaiah:

> *Comfort, O comfort my*
> *people,*
> *says your God.*
> *Speak tenderly to Jerusalem,*
> *and cry to her*
> *that she has served her term,*
> *that her penalty is paid,*
> *that she has received from the*
> *Lord's hand*
> *double for all her sins.* (40:1-2)

In the time of great stress and evil, the suffering ones are reminded that God's word remains powerful and dependable. The promises and purposes of God will not be defeated.

> *But you, Israel, my servant,*
> *Jacob, whom I have chosen,*
> *the offspring of Abraham, my*
> *friend;*
> *you whom I took from the ends*
> *of the earth,*
> *and called from its farthest*
> *corners,*
> *saying to you, "You are my*
> *servant,*
> *I have chosen you and not*
> *cast you off";*
> *do not fear, for I am with*
> *you,*
> *do not be afraid, for I am your*
> *God;*
> *I will strengthen you, I will help*
> *you,*
> *I will uphold you with my*
> *victorious right hand.* (41:8-10)

The preacher/poet moves into the despair and depression of his people, not with a program or blueprint of a new society, but a vivid vision of a new time, a new day. With chapter 42 we see this vision in a new and different literary format called the "servant songs." (42:1-4; 49:1-6; 50:4-9; 52:13—53:12) These songs, four in number, have much in common with the rest of Isaiah but they also contain a new and somewhat mysterious vision of the future, focused on the anonymous servant. This mysterious servant is described in some detail, but never clearly identified.

The servant song with which Christians are the most familiar is the one of our text, the fourth servant song. Though the words may be familiar, one has the feeling we are not so comfortable with their meaning or content. So to make both of our tasks a bit easier, open your Bibles to this section of Isaiah and follow along as I attempt a brief explanation.[2]

Note first of all the dramatic and surprise announcement at the beginning of this song. God speaks these astonishing words:

> *See, my servant shall prosper;*
> *he shall be exalted and lifted*
> *up,*
> *and shall be very high.* (v. 13)

Here the servant seems to be identified as the people of Israel. They are to experience a tremendous reversal in their future. They are to be successful; looked up to; regarded as "somebody!" That is startling news for these people living under the power and yoke of Babylon. It is also surprising news because there is absolutely nothing attractive about this servant of God. How can this plant (Israel) grow into anything important, "being a root out of dry ground." Listen to this description:

> *Just as there were many who*
> *were astonished at him*
> *— so marred was his*
> *appearance, beyond*
> *human semblance,*
> *and his form beyond that of*
> *mortals —*

so he shall startle many
nations . . .
he had no form or majesty that
we should look at him,
nothing in his appearance that
we should desire him.
He was despised and rejected by
others,
a man of suffering and
acquainted with infirmity;
and as one from whom others
hide their faces
he was despised, and we held
him of no account. (52:14—53:12)

Could there be a more uprising beginning? But it was not unlike the beginning of one called Jesus, about whom it was said, "Can any good thing come out of Nazareth?" The preacher doesn't mince words in his description of this suffering, lonely and most unlikely servant of God.

But then he goes on to share the most startling news of all in these memorable words:

Surely he has borne our
infirmities
and carried our diseases;
yet we accounted him stricken,
struck down by God, and
afflicted.
But he was wounded for our
transgressions,
crushed for our iniquities;
upon him was the punishment
that made us whole,
and by his bruises we are
healed.
All we like sheep have gone
astray;
we have all turned to our own
way;
and the Lord has laid on him
the iniquity of us all. (vv. 4-6)

The suffering servant bears the consequences of sin. Now that is a new revelation. All faithful believers understand that sin brings suffering. We remember how the friends of Job reminded him of that basic teaching. But the news in this great text is that the suffering one is suffering, not for his own sins, but because of the sins of others and the punishment which results from them.

This suffering, due to the punishment of sin, is transferred to the servant by God, for we are told, "he is stricken and smitten by God." It is evil doing that is behind the suffering, but because of God's involvement, this suffering becomes the means of reconciliation and restoration — "and with his stripes we are healed."

According to this song, suffering can have a redemptive purpose. God can use suffering for redemption and reconciliation. Not all suffering has this positive result and there is certainly nothing automatic about it. As we all well know, suffering can and has produced bitterness, frustration and despair.

It is clear that in this suffering servant song, that which gives redemptive power and meaning to suffering is the involvement of God. Usually we identify suffering with God's absence, but not in this song. Here the suffering one is carrying out a purpose with which God is identified. We read this remarkable conclusion to this song:

> *Yet it was the will of the Lord*
> *to crush him with pain.*
> *When you make his life an*
> *offering of sin . . .*
> *because he poured out himself to*
> *death,*
> *and was numbered with the*
> *transgressors;*
> *yet he bore the sin of many,*
> *and made intercession for the*
> *transgressors. (vv. 10-12)*

66

These concluding verses to this servant song tell us that this servant was not just somebody in the wrong place at the wrong time. Rather his suffering was identified with the purpose of God. The intention here is not God punishing, but God saving. The servant's suffering happened within the suffering of God.[3]

We can see now why the nation of Israel has been identified as this "suffering servant of God." It reaffirms the fact of Israel being called by God for a special purpose. In its tragic history, Israel drinking the cup of suffering, becomes the way of salvation for Jew and Gentile alike.

This interpretation has much to commend it, but it also has some problems. Doesn't the suffering servant in our text have a mission to the Israelites in exile? If so how can they be one and the same? And all along we have been hearing about Israel's lack of faith which doesn't fit with the faith of the servant in our song.

Though the identity of the servant is not clear, his purpose is quite clear. It was for the sickness and wrongdoing of others that he suffered and through his suffering others received peace and wholeness.

We also know that this great text, with all its problems and questions, has exerted a strong influence on our Christian faith. Later on in the Easter season, we will hear the story of Philip interpreting this very text to the Ethiopian eunuch. The Ethiopian wanted to know the identity of Isaiah's "suffering servant." Philip tells him it is Jesus!

There is also strong indication that Jesus "who came not to be served but to serve and give his life as a ransom for many," (Mark 10:45) was strongly influenced by this servant song text.

Jesus saw his whole life as an act of redemptive obedience to God. Willingly he walked the path of suffering. Willingly he wore the crown of thorns and the purple mantle. Those who looked upon him in misery and woe might well have remembered the words of the prophet, "There is no form or comeliness that we should desire him."

He did not lose his life; he gave it! Here is the redeeming sacrifice. Here is the sacrificial lamb. Here is the Good Shepherd who did not desert his flock, even in the face of death. This is what the cross of Christ is all about. In light of the awful story of the Holocaust, Jesus gets into the car of suffering with us!

In our journey to the cross we have heard many examples of the power of sin becoming visible in the lives of faithless people: the evil times that brought the judgment of the flood; the lies that Abraham told; the story of the Promised Land becoming the land of greed and injustice. Even in exile, the people of God were seduced by the glories and wonders of Babylon, forgetting their homeland and the God who had called them. We heard this tragic history of evil and suffering described in these words:

> *All we like sheep have gone astray;*
> *we have turned every one to his*
> *own way.* (v. 6).

It is our history, too!

It is the old refrain of our lives enunciated so dramatically and emotionally by the apostle Paul, "I do not understand my own actions. For I do not do what I want, but I do the very thing I hate ... Who will deliver me from this body of death?" (Romans 7:15-24)

But against this scary history of sin and evil stands the steadfast love of our faithful God. Our sins are great. We have strayed far from the way. Our garments are dirty. We may have tried to ignore or even bury this "steadfast love" under years of prayerlessness and neglect, under things and more things. But try as we might, here is a love that we can't destroy. Where human love forsakes us, this love never fails. Here is the sacrifice for our sin.

"God has laid on him the iniquity of us all and by his stripes we are healed."

Were the whole realm of nature mine,
That were a tribute far too small;
Love so amazing, so divine,
Demands my soul, my life, my all.[4]

---

[1]Larry Trachte, now a college chaplain, was the intern who shared this story with me.

[2]Gerhard von Rad, *Old Testament Theology, Volume II,* (Harper and Row, 1965), pp. 250-262. The author begins this section of study with this succinct observation, "The Servant Songs are discussed separately, perhaps because we cannot fully understand them."

[3]Bernard W. Anderson, *Understanding The Old Testament,* (Prentice-Hall, 1957), pp. 415-429.

[4]"When I survey this Wondrous Cross," *Lutheran Book of Worship,* (Minneapolis, Augsburg Publishing, 1978), #482.

Easter: The Festival Of Joy

In the book of Proverbs we read: "A glad heart makes a cheerful countenance, but by sorrow of the heart the spirit is broken." A better translation says it more plainly: "A cheerful heart is good medicine, but a downcast spirit dries up the bones." The issue is also clearly stated by the preacher in Ecclesiastes: "For everything there is a season, and a time for every matter under heaven: ... A time to weep and a time to laugh." In the gospel of Matthew this very clear reminder by our Lord: "Do not look dismal, like the hypocrites."

Webster tells us that "laugh" is the general word for the sounds made in expressing mirth and amusement. But it seems that religious people in particular are quite suspicious of mirth and amusement. H. L. Menchen once defined Puritanism as "the haunting fear that someone, somewhere, may be happy." There seems to be in many Christians a strong feeling that God is more pleased with sorrow than with joy. Too many of us, I fear, are suspicious of any happy piety and feel much safer among the gloomy believers.

So I am delighted that as we celebrate the joyous festival of Easter, we do it through some of the most joy-filled words in the Old Testament. We don't know for certain, but the words of our text seem to be describing a coronation banquet in which God is enthroned as ruler. This is a happy, joyful occasion.

This good news comes on the heels of some very bad news. The prophet had been giving a graphic description of the darkness and gloom in the lives of God's people, because of their sin. There had been much desolation and sorrow because God's chosen ones continued to transgress the covenant God had made with them. When God pronounced the judgment that all must face, Isaiah tells us that it was a time when "all joy has reached its eventide." Yes, it was a time when all joy was ended and there were no more happy banquets with wine and song.

But a completely different note is sounded in our Easter text. Here the author looks forward to the return of joy in the coming future banquet which will be for all people. At this time sorrow will be turned into joy. Hear again some of the rich promises contained in the menu of this great feast that ushers in God's reign over the re-created world:

> On this mountain the Lord of hosts
> will make for all peoples
> a feast of rich food, a feast of well-aged wines
> of rich food filled with marrow,
> of well-aged wines strained clear.

It is a good thing these words are in the Bible, otherwise I would be afraid to use them because they sound so worldly and secular. Here Isaiah is using such earthly symbols as "rich food and wine that is well matured" to describe the salvation in store for the people of God. Visions of plates heaped high with broiled shrimp chased down with wine so clear and crisp and mellow that it is unbelievable and of course all followed by a rich, heavy, chocolate dessert, dance before my eyes!

For salvation to be described in this fashion is still a difficult thing for me to accept. The Christ picture that I grew up with and the one that still has a great hold on me, is the Lenten Christ — Christ, "The Man of Sorrows." This, of course, is a one-sided picture and therefore a distortion. It is very doubtful that Jesus could have been a gloomy person, else children would not have come to him, because children avoid gloomy people.

Can you imagine a solemn, somber Jesus describing a camel going through the eye of a needle, or the very serious and respectable folk busily and soberly engaged in the very serious and somber business of "straining out gnats and swallowing camels?" Surely there must have been a hint of a smile about his lips as Christ talked about feeding pearls to the hogs? As a former hog farmer, that comes through to me as being some pretty expensive feed, and I wonder how many necklaces it would take to make a shovel full. Then there is that ridiculous picture of the person with the tweezers looking for a sliver in the eye of his brother, while all the time there is a big railroad tie sticking out of his own eye.

In an important and useful book *The Primacy of the Spoken Word,* the author has an especially delightful chapter titled "Robust World-Joyfulness." Although he did not have this Isaiah text in mind, these words surely capture its essence:

> *The whole creation, flora and fauna, human brothers and sisters, wife and children, music, food, sex, drink, all call for us to sing the Maker's praise. A famous verse often ascribed to Luther encapsulates this: "Wer liebt nicht Weib, Wein, und Gesand, er bleibt ein Naar sein Leben land" (whoever does not love wife, wine, and song, remains a fool his whole life long).*

Later on in this chapter Dr. Wietzke goes on to say: "Can we in good conscience really accept the material order as the proper and only sphere of godly piety, and embrace it with rejoicing? Christ does not wish to turn our festival into carnivals but neither does he desire that they become fasts."[1]

Too often the charge against Christianity has been that it took all the light, zest and joy out of living. One fears that too many of us see the faith as making us do all the things we don't want to do and to give up all the things we like to do. There is an old Rabbinic saying that is a healthy reminder for most of us and it goes like this: "A person will have to give an account on judgment day for every good thing that he might have enjoyed, and did not."

Joyful hearts and the Christian faith go together. Joy gives evidence of the security that our faith delivers. Joy and sorrow can live together. Laughter and compassion are compatible. It has been rightly said that "the opposite of joy is not sorrow, but unbelief." (Weatherhead) To experience joy and to be able to laugh means that we are able to see beyond the present, changing events. Joy sees these events in the power of a good and gracious God who tells us that these events are never the last word. Our text reminds us:

> ... *The Lord of hosts will make for all peoples*
> *a feast of rich food, a feast of well-aged*
> *wines* ...

The joy of a Christian does not mean we deny the tears that go with living, but our joy is a way of affirming something that is deeper than tears.

The words of Isaiah go on to tell us that all will be joy because:

> *God will destroy on this mountain*
> *the shroud that is cast over all peoples,*
> *the sheep that is spread over all nations;*
> *He will swallow up death forever.* (v. 7)

We are told that God will take away death, that veil of mourning that covers the whole world. Death swallows up people in the grave, but will in turn be swallowed up. Here is the real reason for sorrow being turned into joy. The curse of Genesis is reversed:

> *By the sweat of your face*
> *you shall eat bread*
> *until you return to the ground,*
> *for out of it you were taken;*
> *you are dust*
> *and to dust you shall return.* (3:19)

74

Death is all around us. We are living today, tomorrow death may overtake us. There is a familiar symbol of the hourglass with its sand slowly trickling out. That is our life, slowly ebbing away till it ends in death.

Remember the familiar prayer that most of us learned at our mother's knee — the ending of it goes like this: "If I should die before I wake ..." this should be changed to: "When I die ..." That would be a more realistic version, because the highway for death is the busiest highway in the world:

> *If ... all the dying were done in the open with the dead to be looked at, we would never have it out of our minds ... We get no grasp of the enormity of scale. There are three billion of us on the earth, and all three billion must be dead on schedule, within this lifetime. The vast majority, involving something over 50 million of us each year, takes place in relative secrecy ... Less than half a century from now, our replacements will have more than doubled the numbers. It is hard to see how we can continue to keep the secret, with such multitudes doing the dying.[2]*

Death is not some kind of flaw which we are ultimately going to repair via heart transplants, or get around via the quick-freeze method. Death is not some kind of puzzle we are ultimately going to solve. Neither is death pretty. I have seen noble deaths, but I could never describe death as being beautiful. Death remains the dreaded enemy. I think it is the visible evidence of the evil we are all caught up in, and eventually we become its victim. The psalmist writes, "In the midst of life we are in death." So the first prayer many of us learned is a very realistic prayer.

The reason death is such a well-kept secret is because of our fear of it. We don't like to talk about unpleasant things so the subject of death is taboo in too many of our churches. It seems that the more affluent and prosperous we become, the more fearful we are of death. Death means the end of all the toys we have accumulated. Others fear death because it may not be the end, but rather the beginning — the beginning of judgment. Others of us may not fear death so much as we do the process of dying.

I was a parish pastor for nearly 20 years. I have probably preached at least 300 funeral sermons. One of the fringe benefits of being a parish pastor is having the opportunity to rehearse one's own death many, many times. I have had a lot of personal contact with the aging and the dying process. It helps some to joke about it — to tell funny stories. But not much! One can't laugh away the matter of dying. I have been with too many people who haven't handled the dying business very well so it is hard for me to avoid the big question: "How will I handle it?" For these reasons many psychiatrists believe that death is at the bottom of all human anxieties. The poet paints a picture of these human apprehensions of death in these moving words, ". . . crazed we come and coarsened we go our wobbling way; there's a white silence of antiseptics and instruments at both ends, but a babble between and a shame surely. O show us the route of hope . . ." (Auden)

That is why Easter is the festival of joy. It shows us the way of hope. In our Old Testament text we already have a hint of the great hope in the promise that "God will swallow up death." This is an amazing insight because for the greater part of their history the people of God had no real hope in life after death. But here we have an inspired prophet who has the vision and daring to proclaim a time when this great enemy of death will be defeated.

We are told in words that we have heard at many a funeral, "Then the Lord God will wipe away the tears from all faces." This has been called a "tear-drenched" world and so it is. We can't begin to comprehend the tears that have been shed. Who can imagine a time and a place when:

> *He will wipe every tear from their eyes.*
> *Death will be no more;*
> *Mourning and crying and pain*
> *   will be no more,*
> *For the first things have passed away.* (Revelation 21:3-4)

76

Christians see this Old Testament vision of the future fulfilled in the resurrection of Jesus Christ. With Christ's resurrection we believe with the apostle Paul that "the last enemy to be destroyed is death."

"Roll up the curtain and let the light shine in" said an old man as he lay dying in a darkened room surrounded by his children. They did and as the light filtered into the room, the old saint began to sing:

> *I know that my Redeemer lives,*
> *What comfort this sweet sentence gives!*
> *He lives, He lives, who once was dead;*
> *He lives the ever-living head!*
>
> *He lives, all glory to his name*
> *He lives, my Savior, still the same;*
> *What joy this blest assurance gives;*
> *I know that my Redeemer lives!*[3]

Yes, Easter is the festival of joy. That is why an unhappy Christian is a contradiction in terms. Easter tells us there is life and where there is life there is hope. Where there is hope, there is joy and laughter. We can keep celebration alive in our lives and our congregations. We don't have to become cynical and depressed in the face of the many problems of our time. We can throw ourselves into the thick of life with exuberance and great expectations knowing that we are sustained by the power and presence of God. We have something to live for. We can share in Christ's risen life. That Divine energy which at first took Christ out of the grave, is available still — available not only at our journey's end to save us in the hour of death, but available here and now to help us live — to live meaningfully and joyfully. This is the day of joy. We have something to live for.

Thanks be to God who gives us the victory through our Lord, Jesus Christ. Amen.

[1] Walter R. Wietzke, *The Primacy of the Spoken Word,* Augsburg, 1988, p. 159.

[2] Lewis Thomas, *The Lives of a Cell,* Bantam, 1980, pp. 113-116.

[3] "I Know That My Redeemer Lives," *Lutheran Book of Worship,* Augsburg, 1978, #352.

Great Grace
Was Upon Them!

Let us pray: Lord, help us to be faithful in our devotion and worship during these tempting days of spring and summer. Light within our hearts the flame of gratitude that in this complaining and selfish world our light may shine. In the power of your love, enable us to tell the difference between desires and necessities; between enough and too much; between making a living and making a life. Help us to follow your Son in the freedom from the idolatry of things. In Christ's name. Amen.

I am glad you are here! You know the first Sunday after Easter used to be known as "Low Sunday." Unfortunately the liturgical significance of this "naming" was gradually replaced by the reality of the day. The Sunday after Easter became (and remains) a Sunday low in attendance and spirit.

Our problem has been described in these words:

> *The problem, though, is that around most parishes, the summer is far from an electric period of anticipation. The plugs are pulled on many programs, the pace of activities relaxes and life of the congregation adjusts to the languid rhythm of leisure and vacations. ... Instead of breathing in the wild wind of the Spirit, the church goes on a respirator until the fall comes to resuscitate it.* [1]

But since you are here and since we have been hearing these past Sundays that "we don't have to stay the way we are," maybe the unfortunate custom of the summer slump can also be changed! After all, this is the beginning of the Easter season! I know that Easter tempts us with cheap grace with its popular focus on bunny rabbits and early spring flowers. But Easter is more than just a happy ending to a tragic story. Easter is power — power of the presence of the resurrected Christ. Yes, Easter has to do with eternity, but Easter also has to do with everyday living. In the light of that, do our beautiful choirs need to be disbanded? Should nice weather erode away our Sunday commitment to worship? Should our joyful response "He is risen" be so easily silenced by our absence?

You are here. I am here. Let's resolve to change the summer slump into summer excitement. Maybe we won't have worship involvement and participation on these Sundays in Easter like we had on Easter day, but we are going to work at it. You are going to continue to come. You are going to invite your absent neighbors. I am going to work very hard to preach sermons that will be hard for you to miss or forget. We are not going to roll over and play dead before the summer slump.

We don't have to stay the way we are!

This renewed dedication will be encouraged by spending these next six Sundays in the biblical book called "The Acts of the Apostles." This remarkable document is the second volume of a two-volume work by a Gentile physician named Luke. In his first book, we have beautiful stories such as the Good Samaritan and the Prodigal Son. But in "the Acts of the Apostles" or "Acts of the Holy Spirit" or maybe an even more understandable title would be, "Acts of the Risen Jesus," we have important information about the beginning of the church.

A New Testament scholar describes it in this fashion:

No one before Luke and no one after him took this daring
step and told the story of the church as the continuation

of the story of Jesus ... we are justified in calling his work a History of Salvation, *with the subtitles "From Jesus to Paul," "From Jerusalem to Rome," and "From Jews only to Gentiles Also."*[2]

Luke is not only a physician but a historian. For him history is the story of the living God guiding the histories of all people and nations to their fulfillment in Christ.

Here we see in action, the "new covenant" prophesied by Jeremiah. Before, God's chosen people have all been of the Jewish community; but now Gentiles also belong to the people of God and the church becomes their (our) home. Now the privileges, promises and responsibilities that once belonged to Israel also belong to us. In this exciting book of trials, riots, persecutions and shipwrecks, we have the amazing growth and expansion of the Christian Church. Moving into the book of Acts is like moving into a different world. Here we have evidence that God's people "do not have to stay the way they are."

Yes, with the resurrection of Jesus Christ, a new era has dawned. One of the first results, prompted by the powerful preaching of a "changed" Peter, is a mission congregation called into being by God. So this is powerful stuff we are dealing with. People's lives were changed. They became different, new, vital people.

And the world wasn't too happy with them.

The power people, the people in control, were getting nervous about this new movement. After all these were just ordinary, common people who were creating all this commotion. The authorities couldn't understand it. The only explanation they could come up with was that these people had been with Jesus. That really made them anxious, because they thought they had taken care of Jesus on Golgotha.

They told this young congregation to "shut up and shut down." Remember, not everybody likes Jesus. So Luke doesn't give us a romantic or idealized picture of the church. He sees the church under the divine guidance and protection of God, but also always under the cross. Later on in this book, the suffering destiny of the church is clearly expressed in these words from Missionary Paul, "It is through many persecutions that we must enter the kingdom of God." (14:22)

Because the church is in the world it will experience pressures to conform, just as Jesus did and just as he warned us about:

> *"If the world hates you, be aware that it hated me before it hated you. If you belonged to the world, the world would love you as its own. Because you do not belong to the world, but I have chosen you out of the world — therefore the world hates you."* (John 15:18-19)

So this young congregation is under official notice to cease operations. Before, such a warning would have brought on fear and trembling, but now of all things, it results in a joyous, public prayer meeting. This beginning community of believers responds to threats and pressures, not with guilt or fear, but with prayer. These prayers are not offered to save their own skins nor do they ask that lightning might strike dead their persecutors! They do not pray, "O Lord save us." Instead they pray, ". . . allow us your servants to speak your message with all boldness." (v. 29)

Yes, this is how ordinary, common people responded in the hour of great danger. Hearts that were filled with strong convictions, empowered their wills with even greater strength. A papal envoy once threatened Martin Luther, warning him about his dangerous thinking — that in the end Luther's followers would all desert him. "Where will you be then?" he asked Luther. "In the hands of God . . . then as now," Luther answered.

Luke tells us that this joyous prayer for boldness and courage was followed by a great upsurge of spiritual power. Our text reads:

> *When they finished praying, the place where they were meeting was shaken. They were all filled with the holy*

spirit and began to proclaim God's message with bold-
ness. (v. 31)

It seems like another mini-Pentecost experience!

Yes, this is powerful stuff we are dealing with. We may not be the same when we leave the sanctuary.

This unique community of believers, located in the midst of a hostile environment, do not stay lost in rapture, praise and prayer. They do not remain so heavenly minded that they are no earthly good. Their prayers, as most prayers should, lead to action.

Just as Jesus' words had power to still storms and heal the sick, so preaching and praying has power. It changes people. It moved this congregation in our text to action. Now we really see the power of Easter, the presence of the Risen Christ. Hear again Luke's description of life in that renewed congregation of believers:

> *Now the whole group of those who believed were of one heart and soul, and no one claimed private ownership of any possessions, but everything they owned was held in common. With great power the apostles gave their tes-timony to the resurrection of the Lord Jesus, and great grace was upon them all. There was not a needy person among them ...* (vv. 32-34)

I warned you. This is powerful stuff.

Most of us don't get too excited as long as worship deals with prayers and forgiveness and things like that. But when it moves toward our pocketbook, we become a bit more in-terested and maybe even a little more anxious.

It has been said that the trouble with money is that it costs too much! This person did not mean high interest rates. I sus-pect that money is at the heart of most of the controversial issues of our time. We often judge people by the money they make. Our Lord sees the love of money as one of the greatest temptations. Nowhere was he so direct and specific as he was about the danger of money. He said, "You cannot serve God and wealth."

George Forell says, "This idol is everywhere. Marriages flounder on the rock of money. Families are divided, brothers and sisters do not speak to one another because of quarrels over money. The entire congregation gets edgy when the pastor mentions money in church."

Then why should this new, threatened mission congregation in Jerusalem be so different? Because they had been with Jesus! The power of the risen Christ changed this congregation into a sharing congregation. The power of "great grace was upon them." This "great grace" empowered them to heed the teaching and example of their Redeemer Lord. Jesus gave his followers stern warnings in the strong parables of the rich man who ignored the beggar Lazarus at his gate, and the rich farmer who with his wealth could only build bigger granaries. He commended the widow's penny and told the rich young man to sell all that he had.

Here we have the story of a giving, sharing congregation, living under and by the power of God's grace . . . a congregation united together because God had brought them together, and because of that they had obligations toward one another. This was a radical change. In this congregation they looked at things differently. A new relationship between possessions and people developed. They saw hurting people. They saw people who were beaten down. They didn't say, "that's your tough luck!" No, they responded in love; and love says, "when you hurt, I hurt." Love shares what it has with those who have even less.

Some biblical scholars see this event as an unrealistic idealized picture, or as an unsuccessful experiment in communism. We could reason that if all the houses had been sold, then the congregation would not have had any homes to meet in. It is also hard to understand how a community could live indefinitely by using up their capital. So perhaps the picture is somewhat idealized, but the challenge remains nevertheless. Christians are to look at their wealth in a new way. In 1 John we read, "Little children, let us love, not in word or speech, but in truth and action." In the book of James we read this stern warning:

> *If a brother or sister is naked and lacks daily food, and one of you says to them, "Go in peace; keep warm and eat your fill," and yet you do not supply their bodily needs, what is the good of that? So faith by itself, if it has no works, is dead.* (2:15-17)

In the Bible there is no divorce between spirituality and social responsibility. The vertical dimension of the community of believers — that is, our prayer life, worship and study, produces a horizontal expression. This sharing is not forced, nor is it a condition of entrance into a congregation. Sharing our resources is not to be looked upon as the result of some law, but as a consequence of our faith. We Christians in our giving are not preaching a certain economic philosophy, but we are expressing our Christian love.

Due to the spirit of God, a new social unity becomes visible among the members of God's congregation. We share our blessings. We are self-centered people being transformed into self-sacrificing people. We look at our possessions in a new way. With the spirit of God in our lives we rise above "me" and "my" and act on the basis of "we" and "our."

What we do with what we have, tells the world what we believe. That's what stewardship is. That's why caring for the land is so important. Caring for the land is caring for the people who follow us. Land can't be replaced like a failed business. Once land is gone, it is pretty much gone.

Christianity is about caring and sharing. This Jerusalem congregation banded together because God brought them together and because of that they had obligations toward one another. They were invited to live out God's future now. Twenty centuries ago they were to be a sign of hope to the people around them. It was life beyond prudence and common sense. The community of believers were attempting to live that future which they looked forward to ... where there indeed would be no more tears, poverty or suffering.

That's what this community of believers is all about. We are the people of God's future. We are to be signs of hope to those around us. Under the power of God's great grace, we can begin to live that way now. Amen.

---

[1]Thomas Long, *Journal for Preachers,* "The Road That Leads from Pentecost: Preaching through the Summer," Pentecost, 1988, p. 3.

[2]Gerhard Krodel, *Acts*, Augsburg, 1986, p. 21.

Peter's
Second Sermon

It has been pointed out — many times! — that no aspect of worship has been so generally and ecumenically roasted as preaching![1] The many jokes about preachers and sermons rank next to, maybe slightly ahead of, jokes about mothers-in-law.

Being a preacher and teacher of preachers, I have heard my share of funny stories about bad sermons. Like the one where the student preacher, who just finished preaching his masterpiece, piously asked the professor, "With what prayer should I begin my sermon?" The professor responded, "How about, 'Now I lay me down to sleep.' " Or the Scot lady who, at the end of the worship service, greeted her preacher with this evaluation, "You dinna have much to say and you dinna say it well!" Or, "Your service was too long by one half and it wouldn't make any difference which half you left out." Or, "That was an outer space sermon. There was a lot of it, but not much in it."

So go some of the more popular comments about the foolishness of preaching. Yet the stubborn hope for preaching persists. It may be roasted unmercifully, but no aspect of worship is so generally practiced as preaching. One clear reason for its durability is that the sermon has deep roots in the Bible. Preaching is a God-ordained way of sharing the message of salvation.

Clear examples of the importance of preaching are found in the book of Acts. In this notable history of the happenings of the early church, Luke records eight of Peter's sermons, nine sermons by the apostle Paul and seven more from others. It has been figured out that about one fourth of this important book is made up of sermons.

As you have been hearing, this book is the exciting story of the people of God on the way. But the book doesn't begin that way. It has been said that it is hard to steer a parked car and even more difficult to steer a parked Christian. Well, the church between Easter and Pentecost was parked. Yes, the church was in the twilight zone with the pathetic people asking the pathetic question, "Lord, will you now restore the kingdom?" So they waited. But in the waiting they began to move from apathy to expectancy. Then it happened! Luke tells us it happened with a bang. Pentecost! "All of them were all filled with the Holy Spirit ..." This is why Pentecost is called the birthday of the Christian church.

It also prompted Peter's first sermon. People were asking "What does this mean?" That's a great question. Preachers would like to hear more conversation and questions directed to the meaning of events of the day. It provides the foundation for sermons that deal with issues you want to hear, rather than sermons answering questions that no one is asking.

What does this mean? This question provided Peter with the only excuse he needed for his first sermon. One of the marks of a good sermon is that it challenges the listeners about who they are and what they are doing. In a powerful first sermon, Peter did this. Don't forget, this is the same Peter who was hot and cold, up and down, on and off in his relationship with Jesus Christ. But he now becomes a powerful preacher. It only proves what a good congregation, a good question, and the presence of the Spirit can do to make a preacher look good. We have a great response to a strong sermon — the people at the end of the sermon ask the preacher, "What can we do?" Would that more of our sermons evoke that kind of response.

"What can we do?" Peter tells them, "Repent and be baptized." That was one powerful sermon, because Luke tells us, "So these who welcomed his message were baptized, and that day about 3,000 persons were added." With such preaching and the presence of the Spirit, the early church became less problem-conscious and more mission-minded. The church began to move.

This brings us to Peter's second sermon. It was triggered by the crowd's reaction to the healing of a crippled man. It came about in this fashion. About mid-afternoon, Peter and John were going to the temple for prayers. There amid the splendor of the temple, with its graceful columns, gleaming marble and beautiful purple curtains gently moving in the breeze — in the midst of this beauty and wealth, Peter and John were confronted by a dirty, crippled beggar. The beggar was probably covered with rags and flies. As he had been doing for years, the beggar asked for money.

To this request, Peter gave this classic answer, "I have no silver or gold, but what I have I give to you: in the name of Jesus Christ of Nazareth, stand up and walk." We are told, "Jumping up, he stood and began to walk, and he entered the temple with them, walking and leaping and praising God." The beggar wanted earthly treasures, but he received something far better. In the "name of Jesus, he received healing."

The battle against disease and suffering is one from which there are no exemptions. It is also a most unfair struggle. One of my biggest surprises in becoming a parish pastor was the amount of suffering I encountered. And much of it was so unequal and unfair. Some come into the world with poor health, and their lives are one long struggle with chronic ailments and physical handicaps. But all of us have or will have some engagement with the powerful and persistent enemy called disease. The question that it raises: "What part does our Christian faith play in this battle for health?"

Are we, or should we be, Christian Scientists who seem to believe that disease can be fought only with spiritual weapons? What should we think about the popular preachers today and their so-called healing powers? On the other hand, some Christians seem to believe that their faith plays little or no part in their illnesses and all depends on the miracles of modern medicine. What do you think?

Permit a personal experience. Some years ago, I had a good friend — a man who was a victim of polio. He said he was born too soon, because his polio came a short time before the vaccine was available. His was a severe case. He was permanently bedfast. But because he had limited use of his hands, he was able, from his hospital bed, to conduct a self-supporting business in greeting cards, magazine subscriptions and the like.

He was a great example to me and to many others, in the way he was handling his great suffering. We had many conversations. We talked a lot about healing. He wanted my opinion about going to Lourdes, France, a place made famous for its healing miracles. He got around to asking me if I would conduct a healing service for him. I was quite reluctant. I didn't want to be a promoter of false hopes. But he persisted and I gave in.

With several deacons from the congregation and other close friends we held a healing service in his hospital room. I did not give orders to God that my friend be healed. But I asked for healing, both of body and spirit. So did the deacons. I anointed him as the letter of James tells us. But unlike the crippled beggar in our text, or the paralyzed man in the gospels, my friend did not jump from his bed praising God.

I had to confess that though I wanted his body to be healed, I could not believe our healing service would do it. I also have to confess that many fervent prayers of physical healing have been more notable for their failures than their successes. So I have become somewhat of a doubting Thomas in the matter of instant, miraculous cures. I have never seen a withered arm restored, or a paralyzed person get up and walk.

I do believe that Jesus was a healer and also his close apostles. However, I think it was because of their unique relationship with God that they had powers most of us do not have. For me a miracle is anything that makes God more real in my life. I see healing miracles going on today, but I see them being accomplished through the miracles of medicine and skilled doctors and nurses.

This whole problem was usefully described in a delightful book, titled *Cold Sassy Tree,* by Olive Ann Burns. The main character is a wise old grandpa, E. Rucker Blakeslee, who struggles in 1906 to make some sense out of life. His grandson, Will Tweedy was run over by a train and lived to tell about it. In thinking about his unusual escape from almost certain death, Tweedy asks his grandpa if he thinks he is alive because it was God's will. His grandpa replies that it is not, but instead it is that the boy was smart enough to fall down between the tracks.

To that the boy responds that maybe God gave him the idea to fall between the tracks. Grandpa's response is that the boy can believe that only if the boy thinks that it was God's idea for the boy to be on the trestle in the first place. Grandpa continues by telling the boy that God gave us each a brain and that it is God's will for us to use it — particularly when a train is coming.

The boy then asks grandpa if God wills any of the things that happen to people. Grandpa ponders that question for a while and answers that while life may bully people, God does not. He ends his explanation by telling his grandson that there is much more to God's will than death and disappointment. He tells Tweedy that it is God's will for people to be good and to do good. It is God's will to love one another. It is God's will to be forgiving. "Folks who think God's will jest has to do with sufferin' and dyin', they done missed the whole point."[1]

I still pray for healing. I think we all should. Through word and prayer the sick person is comforted and strengthened. That miracle I have seen happen many, many times. That was the miracle that attended my healing services for my paralyzed friend. His body was not healed, but his spirit was. He continued to be a miracle to many people in the graceful and grace-filled way he handled his paralyzed body. The years have taught me that there can be a victorious faith where there is no bodily healing. There can be strong and glorious — yes, miraculous witness to the grace of God in the midst of suffering.

We are to pray for healing, but not just bodily healing. Christianity does not promise perfect health. Physical healing was only part of Jesus' mission. The primary purpose of Christ's ministry was salvation — healing for sin-sick souls. Sin is and remains our most serious sickness.

So, somewhat bluntly our bold preacher shifts attention from the healed beggar to the listeners. Peter reminds his congregation of their need for healing in the monstrous crime they had a part in, and that was the crucifixion of Jesus. He recalls for them that painful moment when they clamored for Barabbas instead of Jesus; when they chose a murderer in the place of the Author of Life.

But God reversed the evil act of the crucifixion by raising Jesus from the dead. And that brings us to the second point of Peter's sermon. First this healing preacher makes the point that he is not the healer. Peter makes no claim for himself. He doesn't ask for glory, not even for a contribution. The good preacher points people to Jesus Christ and to their own sickness.

Now the blunt message of the second half of his sermon:

> "... I know that you acted in ignorance, as did also your rulers. In this way God fulfilled what he had foretold through all the prophets, that his Messiah would suffer. Repent therefore, and turn to God so that your sins may be wiped out, ... When God raised up his servant, he sent him first to you, to bless you by turning each of you from your wicked ways." (vv. 13-26)

The crucial issue is repentance, not perfect health! The issue is a changed heart, a new direction to lives that have become too focused upon self. Repentance is the attitude that puts God back into the center of our lives.

As you heard during the Lenten season, this is no quibble about trifles. Jesus' theme song throughout the gospels is,

"Repent, for the kingdom of heaven is at hand." When Jesus sent forth the 12, it was not enough to cast out demons and heal the sick. They also preached that people should repent. Next to the resurrection, repentance is the most frequent theme in the book of Acts. Repentance was Peter's message in every important situation.

But one fears that repentance is not the mood of our time. We live in the age of the "no-fault cult," a time when apparently no one is guilty and no moral questions are asked. I am "okay" and you are "okay" although wrong things are being done all over the place. No one is responsible.

It is hard for healing to take place if there is no recognition that something is wrong.

So went Peter's second sermon. So Christianity was spread by the word of preaching. But not just words. People repented and their lives changed. They did not stay the way they were. That's how the early church grew — through preaching and changed people.

May we be so empowered. Amen.

---

[1]Olive Ann Burns, *Cold Sassy Tree,* Laurel.

Christian
Courage

"You will go to prison for six months," said the Judge.
So John Bunyan went to prison for nothing worse than
preaching in the little Bedford Baptist Church. "Baptist"
preaching was against the law. But Bunyan persisted in breaking the law. He told Justice Keeling, "If I was out of prison
today, I would preach again tomorrow, by the help of God."

So it was back to prison. This time for 12 years. And again
for six months. John Bunyan, who gave us the great classic,
Pilgrim's Progress, spent one fifth of his life in jail.

This was not an easy decision for him, to break the law
for the sake of his conscience. John Bunyan was poor. He had
a wife and four children who were dependent upon him. He
had little political clout and virtually no status. All he had to
do to avoid prison was to quit preaching because the law said
that preaching could only be done in the established church.

Martin Luther told the government, "Here I stand! I can
do no other!" John Bunyan refused to give any promise that
would bind his conscience, and because of it, remained a
prisoner for the best part of his adult life.

One wonders how different our world would be if John
Bunyan had given in to the government? One wonders how
different our world would be if more people like the great the-
ologians Karl Barth and Dietrich Bonhoeffer, would have said

no to Adolph Hitler? Isn't Stanley Hauerwas right, when he writes, "Auschwitz began when Christians assumed that they could be the heirs and carriers of the symbols of faith without sacrifice and suffering."[1]

John Bunyan is a good example for our time. Today the temptation is to hand over more and more of our decisions to the government and to believe that as Christians we can get through this life without trouble.

John Bunyan is also a good introduction to Peter's third sermon. Remember last Sunday? ... Peter's second sermon in which he explained that the Risen Christ was responsible for the healing of the crippled beggar — not he or John. Then he goes on to proclaim that all need healing from a much more serious sickness, and that is the sickness of sin. His sermon ended on the strong note for the need of repentance.

You know what happened when he finished preaching the sermon? He was arrested and thrown in jail. You know something else that happened? The church grew by another 2,000 people! In the book of Acts, there seems to be some sort of correlation between courageous preaching (which results in persecution and imprisonment) and church growth. Preachers were in jail, but the church grew!

Let me read to you how Luke describes the arrest of these preachers:

> *While Peter and John were speaking to the people, the priests, the captain of the temple and the Sadducees came to them, much annoyed because they were teaching the people and proclaiming that in Jesus there is the resurrection of the dead. So they arrested them and put them in custody until the next day, for it was already evening. But many of those who heard the word believed; and they numbered about 5,000. (4:1-4)*

The wealthy, aristocratic party of the Sadducees was annoyed by Peter's sermons. First of all they were offended by Peter's emphasis of Jesus' resurrection, because they did not believe in life after death. Since they were wealthy people who lived in comfort, prestige and power, the last thing they wanted was any disturbance of the way things were. It was to their advantage to stay on friendly terms with the Roman government. They were fearful that Peter's preaching would provoke the wrong kind of attention from the Roman authorities.

We know this is not the first time a small group of people, in order to protect their own vested interests, would not listen to the truth or give anyone else a chance to hear it. So for preaching the truth, these preachers spent the night in jail.

I am a preacher who has never spent a night, or for that matter, even a few hours in jail. A text like this forces one to think about that. I remember reading some years ago this comment by Dean Inge, "We are distressed because our churches aren't half-empty; but many of them would be emptier if the gospel were preached in them." To insure my safety and popularity do I water down the gospel?

I know some people who for conscience sake, were arrested and spent a night in jail. They were very fearful and apprehensive. Was this the right thing to do? Will I be forever branded as a law-breaker? What will jail be like? These were some of the fear-producing questions. But the jail experience, for conscience sake, turned out to be much more positive than they expected. It seems that most people who go to jail because of their convictions, come out of that experience with even more courage and determination. More recently, I think of Nelson Mandela who spent nearly 26 years in prison because of his convictions. It seems impossible to even imagine such a sacrifice. Yet his clear-eyed convictions and statesman's-like attitude and bearing, place him head and shoulders above most of the leaders of our world today.

A night in jail didn't seem to do any spiritual damage to Peter and John. The next morning they appeared in court, before the prestigious and powerful Sanhedrin. Weeks before, Jesus had been tried and declared guilty before these same powerful people — people who worked closely with the government and who could expect their decisions to be supported by Roman soldiers.

"By what sort of power or by what name did you do this?" is how this court session began. The court wanted to know how ordinary, common people could heal a crippled beggar and stir up such a positive and growing congregation. The fact that a person had been healed could not be denied. But maybe suspicion could be directed toward the healers so they would be discredited. Perhaps they were misleading people with some sort of magic.

This is the question that triggers Peter's third sermon. Once again he seizes the opportunity to proclaim Jesus Christ. Jesus Christ was not just another human being. He was different. Since his life and death, the world is different. In Christ, through the presence and power of Christ's spirit — living is not the same. In Christ, life begins to make sense. In Christ we experience purpose, meaning and satisfaction. In Christ, living is no longer a treadmill existence of one thing after another. Yes, living in Christ, the world is different, because we are different.

This was sort of Peter's standard sermon. He preached it with boldness. In fact, Peter is an excellent model of a preacher practicing what he preached. Luke tells us that Peter stepped in the pulpit before the Sanhedrin, "full of the Spirit." Have you ever wondered what it is like to be "full of the Spirit?" I don't know all that is involved in being "full of the Spirit," but it certainly means being "full" of courage. You have heard the modern interpretation of the golden rule — "those who have the gold, make the rules." Silver and gold Peter did not have, but he did have a heart full of power and courage, willing to share a message that people with gold needed to hear.

One wonders if Peter remembered as he was preaching, these words of promise and strength by Jesus: "When they bring you before the synagogues, the rulers, and the authorities, do not worry about how you are to defend yourselves or what you are to say; for the Holy Spirit will teach you at the very hour what you ought to say."

We certainly see this promise coming true in Peter. What a change! What a transformation! Peter did not stay the way he was. A short time before, Peter had been afraid of just about any kind of confrontation, especially with the authorities. Before, their servants had so frightened him that he denied his Lord three times. Now, having spent a night in jail, fully aware that he was in real trouble, he boldly confronted his accusers and confessed his Lord.

"Aren't you afraid about saying what you do on human rights?" a South Dakota farmer asked Manas Buthelezi, who had just been driving the farmer's air-conditioned harvester. The South African theologian replied, "If I'd be as careful as all that, I'd become irrelevant." The farmer, himself a member of the state legislature, got the point and perhaps some additional insight as to what it takes to live the gospel in our time.

It is difficult for many of us to deal with tough issues. Most administrations want to keep things peaceful and harmonious. Congregations are no exceptions. "Don't rock the boat." "Keep politics out of the pulpit. Sermons are expected to help us in our spiritual life. Count your blessings preacher and stick to the gospel." So comes the pressure to mute the trumpet.

In addition, many preachers are in an ambiguous situation. We receive our salaries from the very ones whose idols we challenge. Hence the subtle temptation to shape the content of our sermons in ways that court approval. Yes, even to become your pastoral puppy — always smiling, always affirming and never dealing with anything divisive, controversial or serious.

There are no simple or easy answers to these subtle pressures to change the preacher into your kind of preacher. I have heard congregational leaders say about their new, young pastor, "Give us a couple of years and we will train him to fit our congregation." You know and I know, that the preacher worth his salt is the preacher who in season and out of season preaches and teaches the word of God. This means not only "comforting the afflicted," but also "afflicting the comfortable."

Remember what Jesus had to say about John the Baptist's preaching and witness?

> *"What did you go out into the wilderness to look at? A reed shaken by the wind? What then did you go out to see? Someone dressed in soft robes? Look, those who put on fine clothing and live in luxury are in royal palaces. What then did you go out to see? A prophet? Yes, I tell you, and more than a prophet."* (Luke 7:24-26)

Faithful servants of the Word are not in the pulpit primarily to keep the congregational machinery well-oiled and the money coming in. God's word not only soothes and blesses, it also judges and demands. Faithful preachers therefore, are not just to be nice and do nice things, but they are also to speak the truth in love.

Christian courage is not just for the pulpit, but also for the pew. Most of us like to be liked a lot more than we want to admit. It begins in childhood. How hard it is to be different than our friends. We have to like the same movies, music, hair styles and clothes. And it doesn't change all that much as we get older. "What will the neighbors think?" is usually much more persuasive than our pulpits. H. G. Wells said, "The trouble with so many people is that the voices of their neighbors sound louder in their ears than the voice of God." It was said of John Knox, the Scottish Martin Luther, "He feared God so much he never feared the face of any person."

Peter, "full of the Spirit, full of courage," ends his bold sermon with this bold claim:

> *"There is no salvation in no one else, for there is no other name under heaven given among mortals by which we must be saved."* (4:12)

The well-known statement is worthy of a sermon in itself. The circumstances under which Peter gave it should clinch the argument as to his courage. There is no compromising spirit here. Peter, even in front of powerful people who could put him back in jail, had little time for the popular and acceptable wisdom, "Since we are all going to the same place, it doesn't matter what road we travel." By virtue of our faith in Christ and the Bible, we are compelled to see Christianity as something special and unique in the matter of salvation.

Yes, we are to see ourselves as the people of God in a special way. But our unique calling is not to result in pride, but rather in additional responsibilities. "To whom much is given, much will be required." We are here for others. Our God has always had one goal, to make it clear to all people that God loves all people.

> *Speak out, O saints of God!*
> *Despair engulfs earth's frame;*
> *As heirs of God's baptismal grace,*
> *His word of hope proclaim.*[2]

---

[1]Stanley Hauerwas, *Truthfulness and Tragedy,* Notre Dame Press, 1977, p. 83.

[2]*Lutheran Book of Worship,* "Rise Up, O Saints of God!" #383, Augsburg, 1978.

The Church
Reaches Out!

The growth of the early Christian Church has been compared to the way people grow up. Growing up is a difficult process. As we have heard these past Sundays, that was also the way it was with the young church. Growing up produced pain, misunderstandings and controversies. Some of these struggles came about because Christianity was born in a Jewish home. We Christians sometimes forget that Christ was a Jew. We owe much to the Jewish people. The debt should create a spirit of gratitude instead of suspicion, hostility and snide remarks.

Though the church began as a Jewish institution, it was not to stay that way. Old differences and distinctions were not to be perpetuated. The people of Pentecost who became the people of the Way, were called to move across national and racial boundaries. A church on the move is a church reaching out! The human-made barriers between people must come down.

A formidable barrier was crossed by this young growing church in the vivid story of our text. It tells us that the church is on the move. It has moved beyond Jerusalem to Samaria in the north. In our text we hear about the gospel traveling to Gaza in the south. On this well-traveled "interstate" to Egypt, we meet a black man, of African descent. The church

103

is not only reaching out geographically, but it is also moving across racial lines. Not only is this man black, but he is also a eunuch, which means a castrated person. He was only half a man, hence an outsider, who according to Jewish law could not become a member of the "assembly of the Lord." Even though he held the high social position as the Queen's treasurer, even though he was on a religious pilgrimage, even though he was a student of the Bible — yet he was a religious outsider in the "twilight zone between Judaism and paganism."[1] Such is the blindness and senselessness of human-made walls.

However, this outsider is about to meet an insider. Our text tells us:

> *Then the Spirit said to Philip, "Go over to this chariot and join it." So Philip ran up to it and heard him reading the prophet Isaiah. He asked, "Do you understand what you are reading?" He replied, "How can I, unless someone guides me?" And he invited Philip to get in and sit beside him.* (vv. 29-31)

Here is one way in which outsiders become insiders. It comes via the "hospitable spirit." Philip is a hospitable insider. He is not afraid to talk to a stranger! He doesn't make the stranger come to him. Philip takes the initiative. He does it without any hesitation. He doesn't seem overly concerned about what kind of response he might receive. He doesn't wonder what kind of trouble this meeting may get him into. After all, this outsider, this unknown stranger, could become a nuisance, calling him at home, wanting a ride to church and who knows what else? But the hospitable spirit is not afraid of being used. Consequently, Philip doesn't make the outsider come to him. Willingly, graciously he accepts the invitation and begins to share the "good news about Jesus."

I am struck by the fact that this Philip, who was not one of the 12, but one of the seven — a deacon appointed to serve with his hands — is not afraid to serve with his mouth! We are told, "Then Philip began to speak . . ." Another translation makes it very clear, "Then Philip opened his mouth and starting with this scripture, he proclaimed the good news about Jesus.'' This one who was appointed to wait on tables and see to the collection and distribution of monies for the poor and needy, is not afraid to talk about Jesus Christ.

But first he listened and learned that this outsider was searching for something. Most outsiders are. This Ethiopian outsider wanted help in understanding the Bible. The passage he was having trouble with was the same one we were struggling with at our Good Friday service. Remember, the Suffering Servant text from Isaiah 53? Well, in Philip we have a lay person who knew the Bible. He was familiar with this particular text from the prophet Isaiah. It seemed oe a popular and important text for these early Christians. This insider Philip willingly and graciously shared his knowledge of scripture with this outsider.

In his explanation Philip sees Jesus as the suffering servant that Isaiah looked forward to, and for whom the Ethiopian was searching. Hearing this explanation of scripture, that is, the good news of forgiveness coming through God's servant, Jesus Christ, the outsider asks if he might be baptized. Then this wonderful climax to this beautiful story: ''Philip and the eunuch, went down into the water, and Philip baptized him.'' With the Ethiopian's baptism, this young, struggling church reaches out and crosses a very important barrier. With his baptism, the church was saying that neither race nor mutilation can separate one from God or God's community. With his baptism, the outsider becomes an insider.

Here it is Philip, under the power and direction of God's Spirit, who helps to break down human-made barriers. In Chapter 10 it is the preacher Peter who leads the way across these important frontiers. In the moving meeting with a devout soldier by the name of Cornelius, Peter is changed and the young church adopts this life-changing lesson: God's people have no business preaching the gospel to anyone with whom they are not willing to eat. In simple terms this means that Christians who come together at the communion rail also relate to one another at the auction sale! There is equality among all the people of God based on our common humanity. God shows no partiality. What God has created, "what God has made clean, you must not call profane (unclean)."

Yes, the baptisms of a Gentile named Cornelius and a black man of African heritage are tremendous turning points in the history of our church. It shows the power of the gospel bringing down walls that separate people. Under the power of the gospel people don't stay the way they are. Yes, these great stories in the book of Acts reveal the power of the gospel, enabling a young church to reach out. In this "reaching out power" we see the beginning of the fulfillment of that great promise made at the birthday of this young church:

> *"But you will receive power when the Holy Spirit has come upon you, and you will be my witnesses in Jerusalem, in all Judea and Samaria, and to the ends of the earth."* (Acts 1:8)

There is little difficulty in making the connection between our text and that which we call evangelism. Concerning evangelism, mainline churches face three big problems: 1) our backyard; 2) our back door; and 3) our ambivalent attitude toward both.[2] Unchurched or dechurched Americans number 90 million and growing. Our backyard represents one of the largest and one of the most challenging mission fields for the church.

The back door of many of our congregations is far too wide. The shocking statistic for my denomination remains fairly steady and consistent: "for every new member gained by evangelism, we lose two and a half people to inactivity."

No, we don't push the panic button and start offering green stamps in order to get people interested in the church. But neither can it be "business as usual." In my part of the country, Hardees Hamburgers has an excellent slogan that has proven very successful for them: "We are out to win you over!" What would be so bad if that became the purpose of all our congregations, "We are out to win you over."

Remember, we don't have to stay the way we are. There is power to change. That means our congregations can change. Therefore, why can't we begin to create that "shepherding, caring, hospitable, evangelism atmosphere" in our congregation? I am talking about an atmosphere, an environment of evangelism. This means we become evangelists for the long haul and the long term. We are not "instant" evangelists or "three calls and you are out evangelists!" Our Lord is too important for that kind of short term dedication. This kind of evangelism is not interested in manipulation, but in ministry.

The wall between insiders and outsiders remains a formidable barrier for many congregations today. There is the visible barrier of racial and economic distinctions. Too many of us still form relationships based on credit ratings and color. But there are also the more invisible barriers that make for outsiders. In many of our congregations if you are older and married you have a better chance of becoming an insider. But if you are young, single, or divorced, you have a difficult time breaking the "insider" barrier. The years have taught me to be suspicious of any counsel or theology that wants to exclude. Our Lord and Redeemer, Jesus Christ, included. Our faith is inclusive. If I read the New Testament correctly, the only people who are in danger of being excluded from the company of Christ, are those who make it their business to exclude others.

These kinds of walls require reaching out that is not a program but a lifestyle. Yes, a lifestyle that is inclusive and is seen in operation, not just on a Monday evening, but in the shopping mall, the auction sale, the basketball game, the coffee shop, the tavern.

A congregation reaching out, a congregation whose purpose is to win over those who are searching for meaning and purpose, is a congregation that is inclusive, intentional and persistent in its hospitable spirit. But the friendly, open, hospitable witness must also be an intelligent witness. In religious circles today the climate is anti-intelligence. Blind faith and gut feelings are the "in" recommended Christian attitudes. The little boy who defined faith "as believing what you know ain't so" was a wise interpreter of our age. Another interpreter of our age put it this way, "Popular understanding of the word 'spiritual' is that which makes a beautiful sound, but no sense." Eric Routley goes on with this telling analysis: "Most people are as interested in the truth as was Pontius Pilate."

That may be a little strong for our sensitive ears, but centuries ago a Roman Catholic Saint by the name of Teresa was just as pointed and sharp when she said, "From all silly devotees, may God deliver us!" Of course we are not saved by our education. But neither does salvation place a premium on ignorance. Christ in his wisdom said to the woman of Samaria, "You worship what you do not know." Too many of us are in that predicament of fumbling and groping in a kind of theological fog with inaccurate compasses. In such a predicament we can become vulnerable to religious quacks and their oversimplified salvation of half-truths. Our ignorance also makes us afraid to open our mouths because we can't explain the reason for "the hope that is within us."

In our text, Philip asks the Ethiopian eunuch, "Do you understand what you are reading?" He replied, "How can I, unless someone guides me?"

Thus Christian nurture and Christian education become essential parts of our mission. If we are going to "open our mouths," we want to be sure that what comes out is more sense than sound. We are reminded of the foundation words for all Christian teaching and learning by the apostle Paul, "When I was a child, I spoke like a child, I thought like a child, I reasoned like a child; but when I became an adult, I put an end to childish ways."

Education in the biblical truths, in the fundamentals of the faith is not an easy commitment. It means a commitment of time, and it means studying with people with whom we may not always agree. But it can be painful in other ways, because education is a process of growth and change and it is not easy to change. But it is through these kinds of changes that we become people reaching out who are:

No longer tossed to and fro and blown about by every
wind of doctrine, by people's trickery, by their craftiness
in deceitful scheming. But speaking the truth in love, we
must grow up in every way into him who is the head, into
Christ ... (Ephesians 4:13-16)

So in God's power to change our lives, we are going to quit offering excuses for not participating in our congregation's learning program. Rather we are going to get on our own soap boxes and open our mouths to the need of adult education, and by our examples become visible in the opportunities that are offered. We may even begin to think about teaching! It is guaranteed to make us more appreciative of teachers and it is an excellent way to learn.

We do this because 2,000 years ago the "Word became flesh and dwelt among us." The early Christian church made a tremendous impact upon the world. We know from the book of Acts that this mark upon the world was made not because the Christians were numerically superior or that they were so popular and successful. They were neither. They were just a handful of ordinary, average folk who were anything but impressive. Yet, because they were with and under "that word made flesh" — they were different. They had been with Jesus. It was that difference, that change in their attitude and being that made the impact.

That Word is now with us. The time is here for us to add our chapter to this the greatest love story of all time. We will remember not just to live it, but also to be able to tell it. Out of all the witnesses, out of all the glorious company of the apostles, martyrs and missionaries of old — only we are left. It is now our turn, to have the time of our life, reaching out with the greatest love story of all time.

I slept and dreamt that life was joy.
I awoke and saw that life was duty.
I acted and behold, duty was joy. Amen.
— Tagore

[1] Gerhard Krodel, *Acts,* Augsburg, 1986, p. 155.

[2] Durwood Buchheim, from a chapel sermon delivered at a Rural Ministry Conference.

Bridges, Not Walls!

One of the more obscene things that I have seen in my lifetime was the wall that separated East and West Germany. I am not talking just about the wall in Berlin, but the border swath cut clear across Germany. Over hills, through forests, and beautiful farmland was this street-wide, cleared strip of land, sprinkled with formidable watch-towers, barbed wire and the frightening, oppressive border sign: HALT! HIER GRENZE! Stop, here is the border, the barrier, the frontier. Even on the freedom side of that warning sign, one would still experience shivers of fear as well as anger. One could not help but think of all the misery, sorrow, pain and tears this barrier caused for countless people.

I remember with what anxiety we crossed that border. Passports were taken, forms filled out, car and luggage were inspected (including gas tank); there were questions and waiting. These slow, deliberate, anxiety-producing procedures took about an hour. It seemed much longer. Though we were never bothered once we got into East Germany, and the citizens couldn't have been friendlier, yet this oppressive border check cast a certain pall over our entire visit. I remarked to my wife, after going through a similar exit process, that never again would I visit East Germany.

We all know what happened. The wall has come down. The borders are no more. Travel between these two areas now proceeds without any fear-producing inspections. The world remains in a state of shock-surprise at how suddenly and thoroughly bridges replaced walls.

Our text for this day describes an event that brought down an even greater wall. The event is the story of Cornelius, and the wall was the formidable, tradition-built, centuries-old wall between the Jews and Gentiles. The strict Jew believed that because God had little time for the Gentile, there was no reason for Jews to associate with them. This was a deep and abiding conviction. Gentile people were regarded as unclean. Thus the wall between Jews and Gentiles was taken for granted. This is the way it was. This is the way it is. Obviously, this is the way it is supposed to be.

These walls do not come down easily. Many of you recall the series on the Civil War aired a few years ago on public television. Once again we experienced the horrendous cost of the wall between white and black people. Bridges are being built, but this country is still suffering the after-effects of these hate-producing walls between people.

We see this in the persistent anti-semitic feelings that continue to persist in Christian relationships with the Jews. The events of the Holocaust are terrible evidence that the Jews in our world have every right to be suspicious of Christianity. I have never forgotten this terrible, but moving story that I read some years ago, which follows.

It is the story about Mike Gold, a Jew and the philosopher of American Communism. He wrote a book titled, *A Jew Without Knowing It.*

In his book he tells an experience from his childhood in the New York Jewish Ghetto. The story is about one time when he went beyond the Jewish area of the city. There he was confronted by some older boys. The boys asked him a question that he had never considered before. It was: "Hey kid, are you a kike?" His answer was simple, since he had never heard the word before: "I don't know." His next question was:

"Are you a Christ-killer?" Again, never hearing that question, he answered: "I don't know."

Intending to teach this Jew a lesson, the older boys beat him up. He then returned home, beaten and bloodied. Later in life, he recalled raising his battered lips to the ear of his mother and asked, "Mama, who is Christ?"[1]

Unfortunately their history is full of these experiences. Most of us Gentiles have little experience with that kind of persecution.

We who are white also have a very difficult time appreciating what it is like to be a person of color in the country. When they step out of their houses they have to be on guard, on the alert, anxious and suspicious of whomever and whatever they encounter. Their history is full of verbal and physical abuse, demeaning looks, vicious innuendoes — a kind of subtle and not-so-subtle harassment that we whites (especially white males) know little or nothing about. In my town, someone called the police because a native American was judged to be suspicious looking upon leaving a parking lot. In a few minutes his pickup was surrounded by three police cars. In another incident, a black person, waiting in his car in a church parking lot, to meet a friend, was surrounded by police cars and police with drawn guns — again because he was suspicious. We white people would raise holy hell about that kind of treatment.

Women in our society also experience harassment. When they step out the door, they don't know what to expect as they walk to work, go shopping or while at their work places. They can be teased, pinched and fondled because they are women and that is what macho men are supposed to do. In too many situations women are regarded as fair game for whistles, suggestive comments and generally disgusting behavior.

There was a wall between Jew and Gentile in the early history of our church, that created division, resentment, hate and suspicion. It was anything but God-pleasing. Thus our text for today describes a turning point in our church that was as momentous as Lincoln's emancipation proclamation during the days of the Civil War.

113

Like so many significant events in our history, this one too, began in a most unusual fashion and came from a most unlikely person. It began when a military leader sent messengers to Peter. We shouldn't be too surprised that this soldier saw visions, for we are told that he was:

A devout man who feared God with all his household, gave alms liberally to the people, and prayed constantly to God. (Acts 10:2)

This God-fearer, that is one who became attached to Judaism and sincerely tried to follow its teachings, was told in a vision to invite Peter to his home.

While the messengers from Cornelius were knocking on Peter's door, Peter too was pondering a Spirit-sent vision. Like Cornelius, he was on the receiving end of a special revelation. He was told that he no longer had to discriminate in his meat-eating habits — that meat which God had cleansed, should not be called common. While Peter was pondering the shocking consequences of this revelation, the messengers from Cornelius described for him the vision Cornelius had and invited Peter to return with them to help make sense out of all that had happened.

This is an historic meeting. It is not just between two individuals, but a delegation of Jewish Christians entering the home of Gentiles. This is a precedent-setting meeting. It hadn't been done this way before! We get a feeling of this wall-coming-down-change in these words which describe the beginning of this meeting:

On Peter's arrival Cornelius met him, and falling at his feet, worshiped him. But Peter made him get up, saying, "Stand up; I am only a mortal." And as he talked with him, he went in and found that many had assembled; and he said to them, "You yourselves know that it is unlawful for a Jew to associate with or to visit a Gentile; but God has shown me that I should not call anyone profane or unclean." (10:25-28)

114

Peter was beginning to understand that the basic issue was not kosher meat or food, but equality between Jews and Gentiles. Equality on the basis of their common creation by God, this was God's revelation to Peter and it was like another conversion. Peter didn't stay the way he was. In the presence and power of God's Spirit, his attitude changed. This Peter who left his fishing boat in response to Christ's invitation; this Peter who on the Mount of Transfiguration had seen the glory of Christ and heard the heavenly voice say, "listen to him;" this Peter who denied his Lord in the courtyard of the High Priest; this Peter who met the Risen Christ and heard the three-fold question, "Do you love me Peter?" and the final command to be Christ's witness from Jerusalem to the end of the earth; this Peter who himself had experienced the empowering presence of God's Spirit — was once more called on to change his way of thinking and living!

God led Peter and the church into a new way of looking at people. It didn't come easily for Peter. This was a change that was extremely difficult. Eating and drinking with the Gentiles was just something a respectable Jew didn't do. So three times he said no. Three times he was admonished by the heavenly voice. Finally the great truth began to dawn on him that all people, whether Jews or Gentiles, were God's people and therefore equal.

Then in the house of a Gentile, he preached perhaps his most eloquent sermon. It was a sermon that continued to emphasize the life, death and resurrection of Jesus Christ, but in addition Peter made plain the important truth that Jesus is for all people. Everyone is included in the mission of Jesus Christ. Apparently this great preacher planned on saying more, but there was a beautiful interruption to his sermon. We are told:

> *The Holy Spirit fell upon all who heard the word. The circumcised believers who had come with Peter were astounded that the gift of the Holy Spirit had been poured out even on the Gentiles, for they heard them speaking in tongues and extolling God.* (10:44-46)

Yes, the Spirit came to all who heard the Word of God. Here we have direct evidence of God's Spirit coming through God's Word. Peter's sermon was the instrument for the Pentecost experience for the Gentiles. Once again we are surprised by God, for this was certainly an unexpected happening. Now the Jewish Christians who heard the sermon and saw God's Spirit at work were astounded.

Gentiles, who had always been excluded were receiving the Holy Spirit. The conviction that God was only for "the lost sheep of the house of Israel" was being repealed. Their history, which revealed a God who was full of surprises, was going to record one more surprise and it was a big one. No longer was there to be a wall between the Jews and Gentiles. All people are God's people. The bridge is in.

This is a warm story. It is a beautiful story about the crossing of a tremendous frontier. It is a story full of wonderful surprises. There's no applause here for the feelings of hate. There's no support for division. Rather just the opposite is true. We have a Roman soldier running out to give a warm greeting to Peter. We have Peter being warmly received by people he was forbidden to associate with. We see Peter's exclusive attitude changing to an inclusive one. We have Peter preaching an inspirational sermon, with the happy result of the gifts of the spirit and baptism. That is one happy ending!

This warm, beautiful story of people changing and becoming open and accepting of other people — people who are different — has to be one of the most beautiful and hope-filled of all stories about our church. Luke must have thought so too, because he devoted so much space in telling it — much more space than the account of Paul's important conversion.

This is what the church is like or perhaps we should say this is what the church can be like. The church can be, this congregation can be — a place where all people are welcomed and received and honored. This is so because our "God has come to every nation;" this is so because "God is Lord of all;" this is so because "everyone who believes in him receives forgiveness of sins through his name." This is so because we

... you and I, do not need to stay the way we are. We can change. Because of God's power we can bring down the walls that separate us and begin building bridges. There is power to change! Amen.

---

[1] John Powell, *Why Am I Afraid To Love,* Argus, 1967, p. 70.

Wheel Within
The Wheel

In our text for this last Sunday in the Easter season, we are at that awkward time for the new church, the time between ascension and Pentecost. Jesus is gone, but his spirit has not yet come. In this time of waiting, we are told that the first thing the church did was to fill a leadership vacancy created by faithless Judas, a leader who betrayed the movement.

Yes, the very first act of the church had to do with getting organized. So the observation has been made that at first and perhaps even second glance, our text is not particularly inspiring or interesting. Who can get excited about nominating committees, council elections and such things as administration, organization, management and leadership? Those words and ideas seem out of place in this place of worship. Frequently I have heard the same fear expressed in these passionate words, "We are supposed to be missionaries, not managers. The church is becoming just like another business." On the cover of one of our religious journals there is the cartoon of two clergy shaking hands, one saying to the other, "Welcome to our parish where we've brainstormed our problems, prioritized our goals, formalized our strategies and maximized our ineffectuality."[1] Their sarcasm expresses what many feel today about the science of management taking over the church.

119

Remember this old spiritual?

> *Ezekiel saw a wheel*
> *Way up in the middle of the air;*
> *A wheel in a wheel,*
> *Way up in the middle of the air;*
> *And the big wheel ran by faith,*
> *And the little wheel ran by the grace of God;*
> *A wheel in a wheel*
> *Way up in the middle of the air.*[2]

The big wheel represents organizational structure and the little wheel stands for the Spirit of God. There is tension between the two — between God's rule and the rules and procedures of an organization. There are a number of Christians who suspect that the big wheel is getting far too much attention. They have a concern that organization, if it is not the death of, surely it is the enemy of spontaneity and enthusiasm. How can one talk seriously about managing the Spirit, which is like the coming and going of the wind, working when and where it will.''

Yet a high priority for this new church was focused on the big wheel. It seemed to be of great importance to this small group of Jesus' followers to bring the apostolic leadership back up to the number 12. This is somewhat hard to understand because the apostles do not play much of a role in the book of Acts and we never again hear of the new replacement, Matthias. Neither do we hear of any more apostolic elections. When the apostles died they were not replaced. The crucial factor in this special election seems to have been the defection of Judas. That scandal had to be corrected. He had to be replaced. We also remember the 12 had been appointed by the earthly Jesus and sent out to proclaim the gospel. The number 12 was a strong symbol. It brought to mind the 12 sons, the tribes of Jacob/Israel, and so symbolically linked the old Israel with the beginnings of the new church. Apparently this connection between the old and the new was so important that the first item of business was to fill the office abandoned by Judas.

This was done by using the ancient Israelite device of casting lots. We are not sure how this lottery was done. The Old Testament refers to decisions by lot, but leaves us in the dark as to how. Somehow two candidates were nominated for the same position. Perhaps two sticks bearing the names of the candidates were placed in a container which was shaken until one fell out. It seems that this selection via lottery was to highlight God's direct involvement and to reduce if not prevent undue human (political) influence in the election process.

Though this particular election and text may not be high on our interest scale, it does convey three truths that are worthy of our remembering.

The first truth is obvious, but sometimes forgotten, and that is the importance and necessity of organization. Without some sort of structure and organization there would be chaos. This was made very clear already in the book of Exodus. Moses was in charge of a congregation that was getting too large for him to handle alone. We also know it wasn't an ideal congregation. It was a congregation on the move, looking for a building site and it was full of complainers. We are told the members were lined up outside his office door from morning until evening. It was not a good situation. Moses was wearing out and so were the people. I am reminded of one of my favorite old, old stories. It goes way back, coming from the "Amos And Andy" radio series. There was a delightful character on that program by the name of Kingfish. He owned a construction company. One day he received a phone call informing him that his construction company had torn down the wrong building. There was a long pause. Finally Kingfish replied in these words, "Let's both hang up and don't nobody call nobody back!" Those of us who have been in the middle of disagreements and controversies can identify with Kingfish's desire. It sounds like Moses was in a similar predicament. But at this providential moment he received a crash course in church management. The teacher was Jethro, his father-in-law. He said to Moses:

"What you are doing is not good. You will surely wear yourself out, both you and these people with you. For the task is too heavy for you; you cannot do it alone. Now listen to me. I will give you counsel ..." (Exodus 18:13-27)

His counsel was to get help and to get organized so that the burden of ministry might not only be shared, but be done more effectively. Moses listened and appointed and organized God-fearing people to help him. You can read all about it in the 18th chapter of Exodus. This people called by God needed some organization if it was going to fulfill God's mission. So it is important to remember that good administration is ministry. Jesus demonstrated such ministry when he appointed 70 additional workers and sent them on ahead. Paul used his administrative skills in raising money for the Jerusalem congregation. We also remember from the book of Acts that when the church grew in numbers, a special group was organized to take care of the widows and the poor.

Structures are needed for effective ministry. Good administration of those structures is also vital, not only to define goals, but also to reach them. Congregations with their councils, boards, committees and task forces have been compared to a can of worms. The comparison may not be flattering, but it is realistic. We who do some fishing know that the worms will always be found at the bottom of the can in a tight, wiggling, squirming mess. You don't know where one begins and another ends. When you reach in and grab one, it is like you grab a ball of worms. You can't jerk lest you tear the worm in two, but you must exert steady pressure if you are going to secure your worm.

So it is in many congregations, with people involved in different projects, concerns and meetings, moving in many different directions. Yet there is much overlapping and interconnecting which requires organizational and communication skills lest there be misunderstandings and confusion. So it is not a question of organization or no organization. The question is whether or not it is good or bad organization. Like the early church, we too need to take seriously, not only the power of the Spirit, but that things be done "decently and in good order."

This brings us to the second truth, and that is "good organization comes from good leadership." We don't know if Matthias was a good leader. We do know that the early church took great care in selecting their leader. Undoubtedly they knew what we sometimes forget, and that is that the "church goes and grows as the leaders lead." It has been my experience that the single most important factor that influences how a congregation will function, is the nature of its leadership.

By leadership, I mean the "art of influencing people to work for the achievement of individual or group goals." There is no substitute for this kind of leadership. A few years ago in his commencement sermon to the graduates of Princeton Seminary, the preacher said these words, "More churches have been hurt by leadership default than leadership domination." (Ernest Campbell)

Good leaders do not wake up in "neutral" or in "park." Leaders have vision. They are more in tune with challenge than with comfort. They tend to focus more on people than on tasks. They see beyond the day's crisis and budget deficit. Leaders place a heavy emphasis on values and motivation and have a healthy intuition for those intangibles that unify rather than divide. Strong healthy leaders are always thinking in terms of renewal and change. They are suspicious of that which becomes routine, for that means the "rut" is not far behind. Leaders do not push the panic button in the face of conflict; rather they know that conflict and good leadership go together. Congregations need structure and organization, which in turn requires good and imaginative leaders.

But with leadership go many temptations. One of the great dangers in the matter of leadership is that we can forget whom we are following. We see this in what happened to Judas.

We are familiar with his tragic story. We cannot ferret out all the motives leading to Judas' betrayal, but there can be little question that money was an important factor. Apparently money was not a problem in the beginning, else why would he follow a leader who paid no salaries and owned not a place to lay his own head. But money can and does exert a subtle and demonic power. In many instances its power grows slowly but inexorably until one is ensnared in its bondage. This seems to have been the case with Judas. Though he heard about "the imperishable treasure that thieves cannot take or moths and rust cannot destroy," yet the desire for more money grew. Though he saw signs and wonders that Jesus did and was a living witness to his unselfish love, the sin of covetousness would not be arrested. The sin grew. That is probably why he could gripe and complain about waste when Mary anointed Jesus with the expensive perfume; why he could go secretly to the palace of the high priest and offer his services in the now infamous words, "How much will you give me if I betray him into your hands?"

Judas' betrayal for money is a warning to all followers of Christ, but especially the leadership of the church. Under the lordship of mammon our needs and desires become insatiable. I am discovering that the sins and temptations of the flesh have a way of diminishing in intensity with the advancing years. But not my greed. My fascination with the toys of the world grows stronger with the years. I don't lust after women, I lust after comfort and things.

That is why leaders dare not forget the one they are following. Under Christ, leading and loving go together. There is an excellent text in 1 Peter that brings this leadership business into healthy focus:

> "I exhort the elders (leaders) among you to tend the flock of God that is in your charge, exercising the oversight, not under compulsion but willingly, as God would have you do it — not for sordid gain, but eagerly. Do not lord it over those in your charge, be examples to the flock." (v. 1-3)

Our best example of leadership is Jesus Christ. In these important words, he warned his disciples about the perils of leadership:

> *But Jesus called them to him and said, "You know that the rulers of the Gentiles lord it over them, and their great men exercise authority over them. It shall not be so among you; but whoever would be great among you must be your servant, and whoever would be first among you must be your slave."* (Matthew 20:25-26)

For too many of us, leadership means going up the ladder, but leadership for Jesus had a downward beat to it. On his last night on earth, he didn't point his followers to positions of honor, but he pointed them to a towel. The "son of man did not come to be served, but to serve, to give his live as a ransom for many." (Matthew 20:28) Leadership is built on trust, and trust comes through service. Service, not domination. Servant leadership is the stamp of those who bear his name.

So our text reminds us, not only of the necessity of good organization but also the need for trustworthy, serving leaders. In all of this process of leader replacement and selection, we see God's care and concern for the continuity of the church after the death of Jesus. This is the third truth coming through God's word for today.

I am reminded of those great words from 1 Peter:

> *"You are a chosen race, a royal priesthood, a dedicated nation, a people claimed by God for his own, to proclaim the triumphs of him who has called you out of darkness into his marvelous light."* (2:9-10)

In the organization called the church there are to be no distinctions between laity and clergy, men and women, Jews or Gentiles. Because of our new life in Christ, we are organized as a community — a community that lives to make God central in our lives by the way we use our gifts to help others. We know this community of "sinners" will not always handle these responsibilities in the best fashion, and our leaders will not always be the bold, unselfish servants we would like.

But it is and remains a community "claimed as God's own." The best administration is done when we have a clear and confident sense of to whom we belong. It is the faithful God of the covenant who remains the creator and sustainer of our congregations. God, through the presence and power of the Spirit, remains, the "wheel within the wheel." Amen.

----

[1]Richard G. Hutcheson Jr., *Wheel Within The Wheel,* John Knox, 1979, p. 16.

[2]*Ibid.,* p. 1.

Books In This Cycle B Series

Gospel Set

Christmas Is A Quantum Leap
Sermons For Advent, Christmas And Epiphany
Glenn Schoonover

From Dusk To Dawn
Sermons For Lent And Easter
C. Michael Mills

The Spirit's Tether
Sermons For Pentecost (First Third)
Leonard H. Budd

Assayings: Theological Faith Testings
Sermons For Pentecost (Middle Third)
Robert L. Salzgeber

Spectators Or Sentinels?
Sermons For Pentecost (Last Third)
Arthur H. Kolsti

First Lesson Set

Why Don't You Send Somebody?
Sermons For Advent, Christmas And Epiphany
Frederick C. Edwards

The Power To Change
Sermons For Lent And Easter
Durwood L. Buchheim

The Way Of The King
Sermons For Pentecost (First Third)
Charles Curley

The Beginning Of Wisdom
Sermons For Pentecost (Middle Third)
Sue Anne Steffey Morrow

Daring To Hope
Sermons For Pentecost (Last Third)
John P. Rossing

www.ingramcontent.com/pod-product-compliance
Lightning Source LLC
LaVergne TN
LVHW021518080426
835509LV00018B/2555